Excel Functions and Formulas Pocketbook

Excel Functions and Formulas Pocketbook

Ali Akbar

Kanzul Ilmi Press

2017

First Printing: 2017

ISBN-13: 978-1975862596

ISBN-10: 1975862597

Editor: Zico Pratama Putra

Kanzul Ilmi Press
Woodside Ave.
London, UK

Bookstores and wholesalers: Please contact Kanzul Ilmi Press email

zico.pratama@gmail.com.

Trademark Acknowledgments

All terms mentioned in this book that are known to be trademarks or service marks have been appropriately capitalized. Use of a term in this book should not be regarded as affecting the validity of any trademark or service mark.

Ms. Excel is registered trademark of Microsoft, Inc.

Unless otherwise indicated herein, any the third-party trademarks that may appear in this work are the property of their respective owners and any references to the third-party trademark, logos or other trade dress are for demonstrative or descriptive purposes only

Ordering Information: Special discounts are available on quantity purchases by corporations, associations, educators, and others. For details, contact the publisher at the above-listed address.

CONTENTS

Date & Time are very important things in Excel, Excel supports many functions related to date & time. This chapter describes many date & time-related functions in excel.

Note: My computer display date in DDMMYYYY format, so I hope you don't get confused when reading the content of this chapter.

1.1 DATE

Date function returns a serial number that represents the date in date-time form. This function needs a year, month and day parameters to form the date.

For example, you can see pic below:

Pic 1.1 Date function

If the cell formatted as General before the function entered, the cell will return regular date. But if the cell formatted as Number, it will return 42038 which is the serial date from date parameter inserted.

You can define Number format by clicking Home > Number.

Pic 1.2 Choosing format for Number

The DATE function is very important when you need to process a year-month-day value and you want to make single date value from that values.

See table below for date function examples:

Formula	Description
=DATE(A2,B2,C2)	The serial date for data taken from year A2, month B2, and day C2 as argument fro DATE function.

=DATE(YEAR(TODAY()),12,31)	The serial date for the last day of this year.
=DATE(LEFT(A4,4),MID(A4,5,2), RIGHT(A4,2))	The formula to convert string texts in A4 (for example, 20151125) that represents "YYYYMMDD" format to serial date.

1.2 DATEVALUE

Datevalue will return serial date value based on data entered. But the difference with the previous Date function is the data parameter inserted in text form, between quote sign ("")

Pic 1.3 DateValue function

Excel saves date value as a serial number to make date calculation easier. For example, January 1st 1900 will have date serial number = 1 and 1 January 2008 will have date serial number 39,448 because it's 39,447 days after January 1st 1900.

See table below for DATEVALUE function examples:

Formula	Description

=DATEVALUE("8/22/2015")	Serial value from date inserted as text
=DATEVALUE("22-MAY-2015")	Serial value from date inserted as text.
=DATEVALUE("2015/02/23")	Serial value from date inserted as text.
=DATEVALUE("5-JUL")	Serial value from date inserted as text.
=DATEVALUE(A2 & "/" & A3 & "/" & A4)	Serial value from date inserted as text by combining texts from cell A2, A3 and A4.

1.3 DAY

Day function will return the day-th value from a serial-date value. You can enter the serial date as string or number.

For example, if you insert 42653 as an argument, this will return day value 10, because it's the 10th day of the month.

Pic 1.4 DAY returns the day value from serial date

1.4   DAYS

Days function is for calculating the distance between two dates. You can enter the two date arguments as regular date or serial date. You have to enter the end_date first, and then the start_date/initial_date.

Pic 1.5 Entering argument for end_date and start_date

If you click Enter, the distance between end_date and start_date will be calculated and displayed.

Pic 1.6 Distance between end_date and start_date

See table below for Days function examples:

Formula	Description
=DAYS("3/15/15","2/1/15")	Finding the distance between end_date (3/15/15) and start_date (2/1/15). If you want to

	enter the date directly into the function, you should enclose it with a quotation mark.
=DAYS(A2,A3)	Finding the distance between end_date in cell A2 and start_date in A3.

1.5   DAYS 360

Days360 returns distance between two dates, end_date, and start_date with assumption that a year have 360 days, or in other words, it's assumed that

a year = 12 months x 30 days.

Arguments needed in Days360 function are start_date and end_date.

C3					f_x	=DAYS360("01/01/2015";"10/10/2015")		
	A	B	C	D	E	F	G	H	I
1								
2								
3			279					
4								
5								
6								
7								
8								

Pic 1.7 Days360 function

In Days360 function, you can have 2 methods as an argument:

Method	Definition

FALSE or empty	U.S. (NASD), if start_date is the last day in a month, it will be the 30th day.
	If end_date is the last day in a month, and start_date before the 30th day of that month, then end_date will be the 1st day of the following month, or end_date will be the 30th day of the same month.
TRUE	Europe method, start_date and end_date on the 31st will be considered as 30th in the same month.

1.6 EDATE

The edate function returns the date before/after initial date after a month_interval. The parameter for this function are start_date for initial date, and before/after month_interval. Before month_interval will have negative value.

For example, this function edate below will count 2 months after 1/10/15 (my computer using DDMMYY time format):

Pic 1.8 Edate function

For example, if start_date is 15-Jan-15 and in cell A2, see table below for EDATE function examples:

Formula	Description	Result
=EDATE(A2,1)	One month after the date in cell A2.	15-Feb-15
=EDATE(A2,-1)	One month before the date in cell A2.	15-Dec-14
=EDATE(A2,2)	Two months after the date in cell A2.	15-Mar-15

1.7   EOMONTH

The eomonth function returns the date of the last day in a month from initial date +/- month_interval. This function has 2 parameters:

- ⊕   start_date: a date that represents the start date, this is in serial number format.

- ⊕   Months, the number of months before (negative) or after (positive) start_date.

You can see example below:

Pic 1.9 EOMONTH function

For example, cell A2 contain date 1-Jan-15, you can see examples below:

Formula	Description	Result
=EOMONTH(A2,1)	End of the month from one month after cell A2.	2/28/2015
=EOMONTH(A2,-3)	End of month, three months before cell A2.	10/31/2014

1.8   HOUR

HOUR function will get the hour from hour serial number. The argument needed is serial_number for the hour. For example, if you enter argument "11:00:00 PM" this will return value = 23.

Pic 1.10 Hour return value = 23

For example, the A2, A3 and A4 cells have values below:

A2 = 0.75

A3 = 7/18/2015 7:45

A4 = 4/21/2015

You can see examples of HOUR function like this:

Formula	Description	Result
=HOUR(A2)	Return 75% from 24 hours	18
=HOUR(A3)	Return hour portion from date/time value.	7
=HOUR(A4)	Date without time information, will be considered 12:00 AM, or hour = 0.	0

1.9   ISOWEEKNUM

The isoweeknum function returns ISO value from week number of a date. You just have to insert date argument, in string format or serial format. You can see the example below:

Pic 1.11 ISOWeeknum display week number of a date

1.10 MINUTE

The minute function returns minute value from time's serial number. The argument is time's serial number. For example, see pic below:

Pic 1.12 Minute value from argument

1.11 MONTH

Month function returns the month value from the date. You can see the example below:

Pic 1.13 Month function will return month value

This is example on how to use month function, the content of A2 cell = 15 Apr 2015

Formula	Description	Result

| =MONTH(A2) | Month from date in cell A2 | 4 |

1.12 NETWORKDAYS

Networkdays returning the work days between end_date and start_date. If the holiday is not a standard holiday, you can insert it in **Holidays** argument.

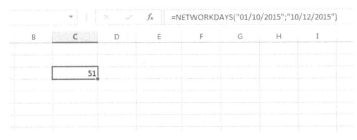

Pic 1.14 Networkdays function

For example, below are contents from cell A2 to cell A6

01/10/2014	Start_date
01/03/2015	End_date
22/11/2014	Holiday
04/12/2014	Holiday
21/01/2015	holiday

Based on data from table above, you can see examples of Networkdays function:

Formula	Description	Result

=NETWORKDAYS(A2,A3)	Work days between start_date (10/1/2014) and end date (3/1/2015).	108
=NETWORKDAYS(A2,A3, A4)	Workdays between start_date (10/1/2014) and end_date (3/1/2015), where the date 11/22/2014 was a holiday.	108
=NETWORKDAYS(A2,A3, A4:A6)	Work days between start_date (10/1/2014) and end date (3/1/2015), with three holidays	106

1.13 NETWORKDAYS.INTL

Similar to Networkdays, but with additional holiday options below:

Weekend Number	Holidays
1 or null	Saturday, Sunday
2	Sunday, Monday
3	Monday, Tuesday
4	Tuesday, Wednesday
5	Wednesday, Thursday
6	Thursday, Friday
7	Friday, Saturday
11	Sunday only
12	Monday only
13	Tuesday only
14	Wednesday only
15	Thursday only
16	Friday only
17	Saturday only

You just enter start_date and end_date and defining what type of holiday to use. You can also add additional holidays if needed. Click Enter, the Networkdays.Intl will calculate the workdays between two dates.

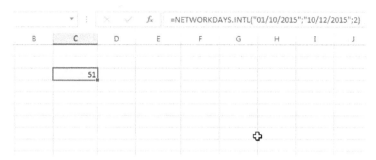

Pic 1.15 Networkdays.intl function

1.14 NOW

Now function is a function without an argument, it just generates current date.

B3				×	✓	f_x	=NOW()	
	A	B		C	D	E	F	
1								
2								
3		03/02/2016 7:54						
4								
5								
6								
7								

Pic 1.16 Now function

1.15 SECOND

The second function will return second value from serial time. Just insert the time, and the second value will be extracted using this function.

| ▼ | : | × | ✓ | *fx* | =SECOND("5:50:34 PM") |

C	D	E	F	G	H
	34				

Pic 1.17 Second function

For example, we have cell A3 = 4:48:18 PM and cell A4 = 4:48 PM. Table below will demonstrate the second() function.

Formula	Description	Result
=SECOND(A3)	Second value from date in cell A3	18
=SECOND(A4)	The second value from the date in cell A4, because undefined, the result will be 0.	0

1.16 TIME

Time function creates time serial value, you can insert hour, minute and second values as arguments.

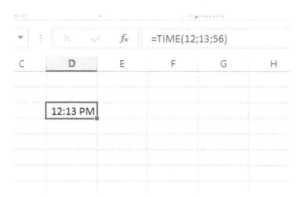

Pic 1.18 TIME function

For example, I have hour, minutes and second value like this:

Pic 1.19 Data used to create serial time value

The table below displays Time function example:

Formula	Description	Result
=TIME(A2,B2,C2)	Create serial time value from hour = 12, minute = 0 and second = 0.	0.5
=TIME(A3,B3,C3)	Create serial time value from hour = 16	0.7001157

	minute = 48 , and second =10.	

1.17 TIMEVALUE

TimeValue function converts string as time value. Just insert time_text argument to use this function.

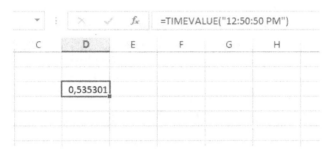

| | : | ✕ | ✓ | *fx* | =TIMEVALUE("12:50:50 PM") |

C	D	E	F	G	H
	0,535301				

Pic 1.20 Timevalue function

Look at this table for more examples:

Formula	Description	Result
=TIMEVALUE("2:24 AM")	Decimal value on time	0.10
=TIMEVALUE("22-Aug-2011 6:35 AM")	Decimal value on time	0.2743

1.18 TODAY

Today function has no arguments. This function generates today's date.

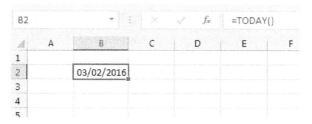

Pic 1.21 Today() function

1.19 WEEKDAY

Weekday function returns the weekday of a date. The result will be between 1 and 7. 1 = Monday, and 7 = Sunday.

You can see example below:

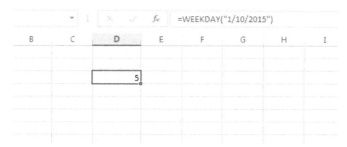

Pic 1.22 Weekday function

1.20 WEEKNUM

The weeknum function returns the week in a year from a date argument. You can see the example below:

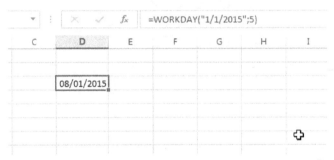

Pic 1.23 Weeknum function

1.21 WORKDAY

Workday function returns start date + workdays. You just insert start_date and number of work days to add. You can see picture below:

Pic 1.24 Workday function

1.22 WORKDAY.INTL

The workday.intl function is similar with Workday, you can customize weekend option. For weekend options detail, it's similar with the options at Networkdays.Intl function. You can see picture below:

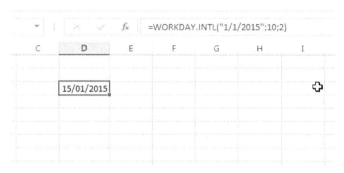

Pic 1.25 Workday.Intl function

1.23 YEAR

Year function returns a year from the serial date value. For example, see pic below:

Pic 1.26 Year function

See table below for other examples, where A3= 7/5/2015 and Λ4 7/5/2014.

Formula	Deskrispsi	Result
=YEAR(A3)	Year value from A3	2015

=YEAR(A4)	Year value from A4	2014

1.24 YEARFRAC

YearFrac function is for counting distance between start_date and end_date in year unit. Just enter start_date and end_date. You can see pic below to see the example:

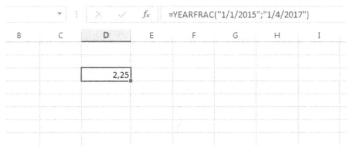

Pic 1.27 YEARFRAC function to count year fraction between two dates

You can add third optional parameter; it has the base used for counting days in a year:

Base	Base for days counting
0 or remove	US (NASD) 30/360
1	Actual
2	Actual/360
3	Actual/365
4	European 30/360

CHAPTER 2. MATHEMATICAL & TRIGONOMETRY

Excel can perform many spreadsheet operations, most of the operations in excel related with mathematical or arithmetical operations. That's why Excel supports lots of mathematical functions, we will discuss some important functions here.

2.1 ABS

ABS function returns absolute value from argument inserted. If you enter a positive number as an argument, it will stay positive. But if you enter a negative number as an argument, it will be positive.

You can see the example below:

Pic 2.1 ABS function

See table below for more examples, where A2 cell = -4:

Formula	Description	Result
=ABS(2)	Absolute value from 2	2
=ABS(-2)	Absolute value from -2	2

| =ABS(A2) | Absolute value from -4 | 4 |

2.2 ACOS

ACOS function returns arccosine value from parameter min 0 to max = pi (3.14). You can see an example on the pic below:

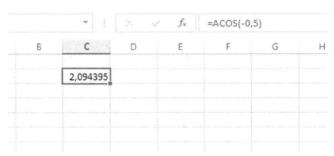

Pic 2.2 Arccosine function

Other examples:

Formula	Description	Result
=ACOS(-0.5)	Arccosine from -0.5 radians, or 2*pi/3	2.094395102
=ACOS(-0.5)*180/PI()	Arccosine from -0.5 degree	120

2.3 ACOSH

ACOSH function returns inverse hyperbolic cosine. Arguments need to be >= 1. See pic below:

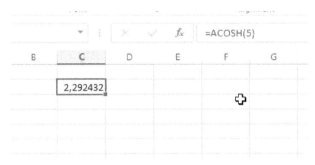

Pic 2.3 ACOSH function

2.4 ACOT

ACOT returns arccotangent or angle cotangent. The result will be between 0 until pi (3,14). See pic below to see ACOT function works:

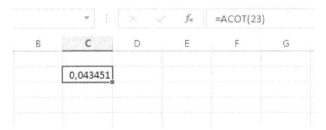

Pic 2.4 ACOT function

Other examples in the table:

Formula	Description	Result
=ACOT(2)	Arccotangent of 2 radians	0.4636

2.5   ACOTH

ACOTH function returns arc cotangent hyperbolic. You can see example below:

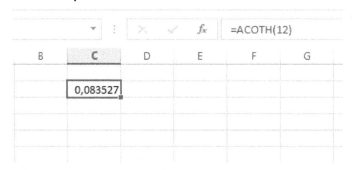

Pic 2.5 Acoth function

2.6   ARABIC

ARABIC function will return normal value (Arabic number) from roman number argument. Just enter the roman number for the argument.

Pic 2.6 Conversion from roman number to normal Arabic number

For example, if cell A6 = mcmxii:

Formula	Description	Result

=ARABIC("LVII")	Returns Arabic number from LVII.	57
=ARABIC(A6)	Returns Arabic number from cell A6 (mcmxii).	1912

2.7 ASIN

Asin returns arc sine from radian value. The range between–pi/2 to +pi/2. See pic below:

Pic 2.7 ASIN value for counting arc sine in radian

2.8 ASINH

ASINH function returns arc hyperbolic sine value. You can enter all number above 1 (>1). See this pic below for Asinh function example:

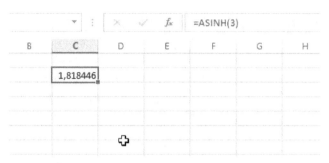

Pic 2.8 ASINH function

2.9 ATAN

ATAN function returns arc tangent from the number in radian. The result will be between–pi/2 and + pi/2. Argument needed is the tangent value from the angle.

Pic 2.9 ATAN function

The table below shows more examples of ATAN function:

Formula	Description	Result
=ATAN(1)	Arctangent from 1 radian, pi/4	0.785398163
=ATAN(1)*180/PI()	Arctangent from 1 degree	45

| =DEGREES(ATAN(1)) | Arctangent from 1 degree | 45 |

2.10 ATAN2

ATAN2 returns arctangent from x,y coordinate in radian, the value between–pi and pi, but exclude–pi. The argument needed just the x, y coordinate.

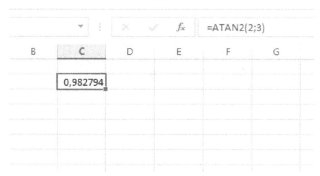

Pic 2.10 ATAN2 function

See examples of ATAN2 function in table below:

Formula	Description	Result
=ATAN2(1, 1)	Arctangent from 1,1 in radian or pi/4	0.785398163
=ATAN2(-1, -1)	Arctangent from -1,-1 in radian, or -3*pi/4	-2.35619449

=ATAN2(-1, 1)*180/PI()	Arctangent from 1,1 in degrees.	-135
=DEGREES(ATAN2(-1, -1))	Arctangent from 1,1 in degrees	-135

2.11 ATANH

ATANH returns hyperbolic arctangent from the argument. The argument can be a real number from -1 and 1 but excludes the -1 and 1. See pic below to see atanh function example:

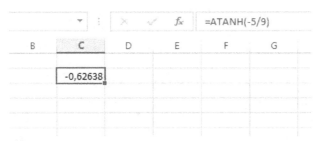

Pic 2.11 ATANH function

2.12 BASE

The BASE will change the number argument to a certain number with radix you define. See pic 2.12 below to see the base function:

Pic 2.12 Changing 10 to binary with radix 2 using BASE function

See table below for more examples:

Formula	Description	Result
=BASE(7,2)	Converting decimal value 7 with base = 2.	111
=BASE(100,16)	Converting decimal value 100 with base = 16 or hexadecimal.	64
=BASE(15,2,10)	Converting decimal value 15 with base = 2 and min length = 10.	0000001111

2.13 CEILING.MATH

Ceiling.math function rounds the number to the nearest integer which is multiples of a certain number. See pics below:

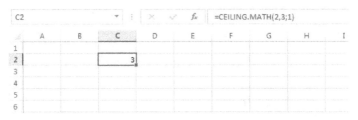

Pic 2.13 Ceiling math for 2.3 multiples 1

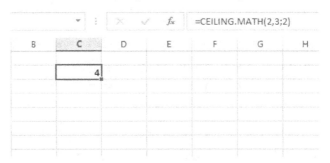

Pic 2.14 Ceiling math for 2.3 multiples 2

See table below for more examples:

Formula	Description	Result
=CEILING.MATH(24.3,5)	Rounding 24.3 to nearest integer multiples 5.	25
=CEILING.MATH(6.7)	Rounding 6.7 to the nearest integer.	7
=CEILING.MATH(-8.1,2)	rounding -8.1 to nearest integer multiples 2.	-8

=CEILING.MATH(-5.5,2,-1)	Rounding -5.5 below, multiples 2 with mode -1.	-6

2.14 COMBIN

Combin function calculates combination using arguments:

n (number)

k (chosen number)

with equation formula like this:

$$\binom{n}{k} = \frac{P_{k,n}}{k!} = \frac{n!}{k!(n-k)!}$$

Where:

$$P_{k,n} = \frac{n!}{(n-k)!}$$

You can insert n and k as arguments, and the Combin function will calculate the combination of n and k directly:

Pic 2.15 Combin function

See table below for Combin function example.

Formula	Description	Result
=COMBIN(8,2)	A possibility of creating two members team from 8 candidates.	28

2.15 COMBINA

COMBINA function returns combination with repetition for some items. See pic below for example:

Pic 2.16 Using COMBINA function

See table below for other examples of COMBINA function

Formula	Description	Result
=COMBINA(4,3)	Combination with repetition for 4 and 3.	20
=COMBINA(10,3)	Combination with repetition for 10 and 3.	220

2.16 COS

Cos function returns cosine value from an angle in radian. This function only has one argument, the angle in radian.

	A	B	C	D
1				
2		Angle Value	COS	
3		1	0,540302	
4		2	-0,41615	
5		3	-0,98999	
6				
7				

Pic 2.17 Cos function

You can see some examples of COS function on table below:

Formula	Description	Result
=COS(1.047)	Cosine of 1.047 radian	0.5001711
=COS(60*PI()/180)	Cosine of 60 degree	0.5
=COS(RADIANS(60))	Cosine of 60 degree	0.5

2.17 COSH

COSH returns hyperbolic cosine from an angle. It has only one argument, the angle value. Look at the pic below to see example:

E3			✕	✓	f_x
◢	A	B	C	D	
1					
2		Angle Value	COSH		
3		1	1,543081		
4		2	3,762196		
5		3	10,06766		
6					
7					
8					

Pic 2.18 CosH function from angles

The formula to count COSH:

$$COSH(z) = \frac{e^z + e^{-z}}{2}$$

For more examples of COSH functions, see table below:

Formula	Description	Result
=COSH(4)	Hyperbolic cosine of 4	27.308233
=COSH(EXP(1))	Hyperbolic cosine of the normal base algorithm.	7.6101251

2.18 DECIMAL

The decimal function returns decimal representation from number argument, based on radix value. The syntax is

DECIMAL(text, radix)

The argument is two, text and radix. Radix must be an integer.

	A	B	C	D
1				
2	Radix	VALUE	Decimal Value	
3	2	1010101010	682	
4	16	14	20	
5	4	3	3	
6				
7				
8				

Pic 2.19 Decimal function

2.19 DEGREES

DEGREES function will change radian value to a degree. You can see pic below:

	A	B	C	D
1				
2		Radian	Degrees	
3		1	57,29577951	
4		2	114,591559	
5		3	171,8873385	
6				
7				

Pic 2.20 Degrees function

See table below for DEGREES function example:

Formula	Description	Result

| =DEGREES(PI()) | Degrees from pi | 180 |

2.20 EVEN

EVEN function rounds the value to the closest even integer. You can see pic below:

◢	A	B	C	D	E
1					
2		Value	Even		
3		1,4	2		
4		4,3	6		
5		2,6	4		
6					
7					
8					
9					
10					
11					

Pic 2.21 EVEN function

See table below to see examples of even function:

Formula	Description	Result
=EVEN(1.5)	Rounding 1.5 to the closest even integer.	2
=EVEN(3)	Rounding 3 to closest even integer	4
=EVEN(2)	Rounding 2 to the closest even integer.	2
=EVEN(-1)	Rounding -1 to the closest even integer.	-2

2.21 EXP

EXP function returns exponential e to a certain number. e = 2.71828182845904, the base of the natural algorithm. Here's an example of an exponential algorithm using EXP function:

	A	B	C	D
1				
2		Value	EXP	
3		1	2,718281828	
4		2	7,389056099	
5		3	20,08553692	
6				
7				
8				
9				
10				

Pic 2.22 EXP functions

Exp function is an inverse of LN function.

2.22 FACT

FACT function returns factorial calculation. Factorial formula is 1 x 2 x 3 x.. . .. x number. You can see pic 2.23 below.

E5				f_x	
	A	B	C	D	E
1					
2		Value	FACT		
3		1	1		
4		2	2		
5		3	6		
6					
7					
8					
9					

Pic 2.23 FACT function to calculate factorial

See table below for other examples:

Formula	Description	Result
=FACT(5)	Factorial of 5, or 1*2*3*4*5	120
=FACT(1.9)	Factorial of 1.9	1
=FACT(0)	Factorial of 0	1
=FACT(-1)	Factorial of negative value will generate an error.	#NUM!
=FACT(1)	Factorial of 1	1

2.23 FACTDOUBLE

FACTDOUBLE returns double factorial of the number. See pic 2.24 below:

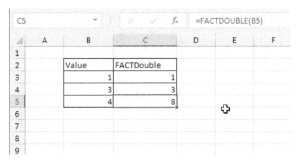

Pic 2.24 FACTDOUBLE function

See table below for more examples:

Formula	Description	Result

| =FACTDOUBLE(6) | Double factorial of 6. Because it has an even number, the double factorial = 6*4*2; the formula is:

n!! = n*(n-2)*(n-4)...(4)(2) | 48 |
| =FACTDOUBLE(7) | Double factorial for 7. Because it has odd the double factorial = 7*5*3; the formula:
n!! = n*(n-2)*(n-4)...(3)(1) | 105 |

2.24 FLOOR.MATH

Floor.Math function rounding number down to the closest integer. FLOOR.MATH(number, significance, mode).

- Number: number to be rounded down.

- Significance: optional, multiplication.

- Mode: Optional, when rounding down negative value, you can define whether toward 0 or away from 0.

Pic 2.25 Floor.MATH function

See table below for other examples:

Formula	Description	Result
=FLOOR.MATH(24.3,5)	Rounding down 24.3, to closest integer multiplication of 5.	20
=FLOOR.MATH(6.7)	Rounding down 6.7 to closes integer.	6
=FLOOR.MATH(-8.1,2)	Rounding down -8.1 away from 0, multiplication of 2.	-10
=FLOOR.MATH(-5.5,2,-1)	Rounding down -5.5 toward 0 multiplication of 2, using a non-zero method that will reverse the rounding method.	-4

2.25 GCD

GCD counts greatest common divisor. The syntax:

GCD(num1, num2, etc...)

Pic 2.26 GCD

See table below for more examples:

Formula	Description	Result
=GCD(5, 2)	GCD of 5 and 2	1
=GCD(24, 36)	GCD of 24 and 36	12
=GCD(7, 1)	GCD of 7 and 1	1
=GCD(5, 0)	GCD of 5 and 0	5

2.26 INT

INT function syntax = INT(number). It rounds number to closest integer.

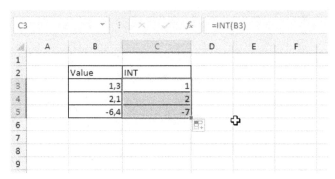

Pic 2.27 INT function

See table below for more examples:

Formula	Description	Result
=INT(8.9)	Rounding down 8.9	8
=INT(-8.9)	Rounding down -8.9. Rounding negative value will make it away from 0.	-9
=A2-INT(A2)	Rounding decimal from cell A2. For example, cell A2 = 1.5	0.5

2.27 LOG

LOG function returns logarithmic from number using defined base.

LOG(number, base)

The first argument is mandatory; it has a real number to find the logarithmic. The base is optional, if empty, it is considered 10.

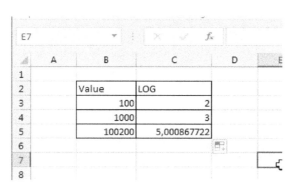

Pic 2.28 LOG function

See table below for more examples:

Formula	Description	Result
=LOG(10)	Log value from 10. Because the second argument not exists, the value assumed to be 10, the result 1.	1
=LOG(8, 2)	Log 8 with base 2.	3
=LOG(86, 2.7182818)	Log 86 with base e (2.718).	4.4543473

2.28 MOD

MOD function returns the modulus. There are two arguments:

n = number,

d = denominator

MOD and INT are correlated by the formula below:

MOD(n, d) = n - d*INT(n/d)

Pic 2.29 MOD function

Formula	Description	Result
=MOD(3, 2)	Modulus of 3/2	1
=MOD(-3, 2)	Modulus -3/2. Sign will be the same with denominator	1
=MOD(3, -2)	Modulus 3/-2. The sign will be the same with the denominator.	-1
=MOD(-3, -2)	Modulus -3/-2. The sign will be the same with the denominator.	-1

2.29 ODD

The ODD function will round number to closest odd number, the negative number will be rounded away from 0.

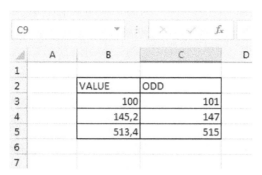

Pic 2.30 ODD function

See table below for more examples of Odd function:

Formula	Description	Result
=ODD(1.5)	Rounding 1.5 to the closest odd integer.	3
=ODD(3)	Rounding 3 to the closest odd integer.	3
=ODD(2)	Rounding 2 to the closest odd integer.	3
=ODD(-1)	Rounding -1 to the closest odd integer.	-1
=ODD(-2)	Rounding -2 away from 0 to closest odd integer	-3

2.30 PI

Pi() function returns 3.14159265358979, it's pi constant accurate up to 15 digits.

Pic 2.31 pi() function to generate pi constant

See table below for more examples:

Formula	Description	Results
=PI()	Returns pi.	3.141592654
=PI()/2	Returns pi/2.	1.570796327

2.31 POWER

Power function equal with operator "^". For example, power (5;2) = 5^2.

Pic 2.32 Power function in excel

See table below for more examples:

Formula	Description	Result
=POWER(5,2)	5^2 = 5x5.	25
=POWER(98.6,3.2)	98.6 ^ 3.2.	2401077.222
=POWER(4,5/4)	4 ^ 5/4.	5.656854249

2.32 PRODUCT

PRODUCT function multiplies all arguments inserted.

Pic 2.33 PRODUCT function multiplies all arguments

PRODUCT function used when you want to multiply more than one value.

PRODUCT(A1:A3, C1:C3) =A1 * A2 * A3 * C1 * C2 * C3.

See table below for more Product function examples:

Formula	Description
=PRODUCT(A2:A4)	Multiply content of A2 until A4 (A2, A3, A4).

=PRODUCT(A2:A4, 2)	Multiply A2, A3, A4, then multiply the result with 2.
=A2*A3*A4	Multiply A2, A3, A4 using multiply operator, not PRODUCT function.

2.33 QUOTIENT

Quotient operator returns integer portion of divide operation result, the syntax is:

QUOTIENT(numerator, denominator)

The denominator is the divider.

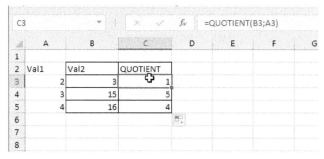

Pic 2.34 Quotient function

See table QUOTIENT and the explanation

Formula	Description	Result
=QUOTIENT(5, 2)	Integer portion of 5/2	2
=QUOTIENT(4.5, 3.1)	Integer portion of 4.5/3.1	1
=QUOTIENT(-10, 3)	Integer portion of -10/3	-3

2.34 RADIAN

Radian function converse degrees value to radians.

Pic 2.35 Radians function

See table below for example, of radians function

Formula	Description	Result
=RADIANS(270)	Radians of 270 degrees	4.712389

2.35 RAND

RAND function doesn't need argument. This will generate a random number between 0 and 1.

Pic 2.36 RAND function

See table below for more examples of RAND function:

Formula	Description
=RAND()	Generate random number between 0 and 1
=RAND()*100	Generate a random number between 0 and 1, then multiply it with 100.

2.36 ROUND

Round function will round value with digits = num_digits. Only have two arguments, number, and num_digit. Here is the example of ROUND function in Excel:

		f_x	=ROUND(5,67;-2)		
C	D	E	F	G	
	ROUND(5,78998789;2)	5,79			
	ROUND(5,67;-2)	0			

Pic 2.37 Round function

If num_digits > 0 (zero), the number will be rounded with digits = num_digits. If num_digits = 0, the number will be rounded up to the closest integer.

If num_digits < 0, the number will be rounded left from a decimal value. See table below for more examples:

Formula	Description	Result
=ROUND(2.15, 1)	Rounding 2.15 to one decimal value.	2.2
=ROUND(2.149, 1)	Rounding 2.149 to one decimal value	2.1
=ROUND(-1.475, 2)	Rounding -1.475 to two decimal value.	-1.48
=ROUND(21.5, - 1)	Rounding 21.5 to with num_digits= -1	20

2.37 SUM

SUM will add all arguments inserted. For example, on the pic below, SUM will add all variables:

Pic 2.38 SUM value

2.38 SUMIF

SUMIF function similar with SUM, but you can give a conditional statement so that excel will add only some values that conform the conditional statement.

| D6 | | | fx | =SUMIF(D3:D5;"<105") |

	A	B	C	D	E	F	G	H
1								
2								
3			Nilai 1	100				
4			Nilai 2	104				
5			Nilai 3	140				
6			SUM IF	204				
7								
8								
9								

Pic 2.39A SUMIF function

For example, A1 to B5 have content like this:

| G9 | | | fx | |

	A	B	C	D	E
1	Property Price	Commission	Data		
2	100	7	250		
3	200	14			
4	300	21			
5	400	28			
6					
7					
8					

Pic 2.39B

From data above, see table below for examples of SUMIF function:

Formula	Descriptio n	Result

=SUMIF(A2:A5,">160000",B2:B5)	Sum of Commission for property price > 160,000.	63,000
=SUMIF(A2:A5,">160000")	Sum of Property price more than > 160,000.	900,000
=SUMIF(A2:A5,300000,B2:B5)	Sum of commission for property price = 300,000.	21,000
=SUMIF(A2:A5,">" & C2,B2:B5)	Sum of commission for property > C2.	49,000

2.39 TRUNC

Truncate will truncate number to certain decimal value.

Pic 2.40 Truncate value

See table below for more examples of trunc function:

Formula	Description	Result
=TRUNC(8.9)	Integer value from 8.9	8
=TRUNC(-8.9)	Integer value from -8.9	-8
=TRUNC(PI())	Integer from pi	3

Excel supports some database operations, although not as advanced as MS Access. You can see many database functions in this chapter.

3.1 DAVERAGE

DAVERAGE function calculates the average from database columns/fields which meet the criteria. The syntax of Daverage function is:

DAVERAGE(database, field, criteria)

The arguments:

☺ Database: a range that contains the database. The first row is the label's name.

☺ Field: Indicate which column used in a function.

☺ Criteria: Range that contains criteria.

For example, you can see content below:

	A	B	C	D	E	F	G
1	Tree	Height	Age	Gain	Profit	Height	
2	APPLE	>10				<16	
3	PEAR						
4	Tree	Height	Age	Gain	Profit		
5	Apple	18	20	14	105		
6	Pear	12	12	10	96		
7	Cherry	13	14	9	105		
8	Apple	14	15	10	75		
9	Pear	9	8	8	76		
10	Apple	8	9	6	45		
11							
12							

Pic 3.1 Data for Function

From data above, you can use DAVERAGE to calculate average below:

Formula	Description	Result
=DAVERAGE(A4:D10; "Gain";A1:A2)	Average gain of apple tree with height > 10 feet	10
=DAVERAGE(A4:E10;3; A4:E10)	Average of all trees in the database.	13

3.2 DCOUNT

DCOUNT will count cell in a database. The sintax is similar to DAVERAGE, as follow:

DCOUNT(database,field,criteria)

With data example, similar as above, you can use dcount to count cell on the database. See table below:

Formula	Description	Result
=DCOUNT(A4:D10; "Profit";A1:A2)	Gain count for apple tree with height > 10	3
=DCOUNT(A4:E10;3; A4:E10)	Count of all tree in database	6

3.3   DCOUNTA

DCOUNTA will count cells that are not empty in database columns or lists. The syntax:

DCOUNTA (database, field, criteria)

See table below for example:

Formula	Description	Result
=DCOUNTA(A4:E10, "Profit",A1:F2)	See record from the apple tree with the height between 10 and 16, and count columns in profit that are not empty.	1

3.4   DGET

DGET will extract a single value from database columns or lists. Based on the condition you defined. The syntax:

DGET(database, field, criteria)

If no records match criteria, DGET will return error #VALUE!. If more than one records match the criteria, DGET will return #NUM!. See table below for DGET function examples:

Formula	Description	Result

=DGET(A5:E11, "Perolehan", A1:A3)	Displaying #NUM! Because more than one records match the criteria.	#NUM!
=DGET(A5:E11, "Perolehan", A1:F3)	Returns 10, because this is the only criteria that match criteria's in range A1:F3.	10

3.5 DMAX

DMAX function will return the largest value in database fields or lists that match the criteria.

DMAX(database, field, criteria)

See table below for example, of Dmax function:

Formula	Description	Result
=DMAX(A4:E10, "Profit", A1:A3)	Max profit for apple and pear trees.	105

3.6 DMIN

DMIN function returns the smallest value from database fields or list that matches the criteria. The syntax:

DMIN(database, field, criteria)

See table below for DMIN function example:

Formula	Description	Result
=DMIN(A4:E10, "Profit", A1:B2)	Min profit for apple trees that match criteria.	45

3.7 DSUM

DSUM function will add value in database fields or lists that match the criteria.

The syntax:

DSUM(database,field,criteria)

See table below for example:

Formula	Description	Result
=DSUM(A4:E10, "Profit", A1:B2)	Sum of profit for apple trees that match the criteria.	397

Excel supports many functions related to engineering fields. This chapter will describe the most important functions.

4.1 BIN2DEC

Bin2Dec will convert a binary number to decimal. The syntax:

BIN2DEC(number)

The argument cannot exceed 10 chars or 10 bit.

Pic 4.1 Bin2Dec function to convert binary to decimal

See table below for more examples of Bin2Dec function:

Formula	Description	Result
=BIN2DEC(1100100)	Converting binary 1100100 to decimal	100
=BIN2DEC(1111111111)	Converting binary 1111111111 to decimal	-1

4.2   CONVERT

Convert will convert the value into one unit to another unit. For example, from m to mile, or from mile to kilometre.

CONVERT(number, initial_unit, end_unit)

Some units supported:

Mass and Weight	Initial_unit or end_unit
Gram	"g"
Slug	"sg"
Pound mass (avoirdupois)	"lbm"
U (atomic mass unit)	"u"
Ounce mass (avoirdupois)	"ozm"

For length:

Length	Initial_Unit or End_unit
Meter	"m"
Statute mile	"mi"
Nautical mile	"Nmi"
Inch	"in"
Foot	"ft"
Yard	"yd"

Angstrom	"ang"
Pica	"pica"

For time units:

TIME	Initial_unit or end_unit
Year	"yr"
Day	"day"
Hour	"hr"
Minute	"mn"
Second	"sec"

For pressure units:

Pressure	Initial_unit or end_unit
Pascal	"Pa" (or "p")
Atmosphere	"atm" (or "at")
mm of Mercury	"mmHg"

For power units:

Power	Initial_unit or end_unit
Newton	"N"

Dyne	"dyn" (or "dy")
Pound force	"lbf"
Horsepower	"HP" (or "h")
Watt	"W" (or "w")

For energy units:

Energy	Initial_unit, end_unit
Joule	"J"
Erg	"e"
Thermodynamic calorie	"c"
IT calorie	"cal"
Electron volt	"eV" (or "ev")
Horsepower-hour	"HPh" (or "hh")
Watt-hour	"Wh" (or "wh")
Foot-pound	"flb"
BTU	"BTU" (or "btu")

For magnetism:

Magnetism	Initial_unit, end_unit
Tesla	"T"

Gauss	"ga"

For temperature units:

Temperature	Initial_unit, end_unit
Degree Celsius	"C" (or "cel")
Degree Fahrenheit	"F" (or "fah")
Kelvin	"K" (or "kel")

For liquid measure units:

Liquid measure	Initial_unit, measure_unit
Teaspoon	"tsp"
Tablespoon	"tbs"
Fluid ounce	"oz"
Cup	"cup"
U.S. pint	"pt" (or "us_pt")
U.K. pint	"uk_pt"
Quart	"qt"
Gallon	"gal"
Liter	"l" (or "lt")

For prefix units:

Prefix	Multiplier	Abbreviation
exa	1E+18	"E"
peta	1E+15	"P"
tera	1E+12	"T"
giga	1E+09	"G"
mega	1E+06	"M"
kilo	1E+03	"k"
hecto	1E+02	"h"
dekao	1E+01	"e"
deci	1E-01	"d"
centi	1E-02	"c"
milli	1E-03	"m"
micro	1E-06	"u"
nano	1E-09	"n"
pico	1E-12	"p"
femto	1E-15	"f"
atto	1E-18	"a"

Pic 4.2 CONVERT function example

See table below to see Convert function examples:

Formula	Description	Result
=CONVERT(1.0, "lbm", "kg")	Converting 1 pound to kilogram.	0.453592
=CONVERT(68, "F", "C")	Converting 68 degrees Fahrenheit to Celsius	20
=CONVERT(2.5, "ft", "sec")	The data unit type not equals, returns error.	#N/A
=CONVERT(CONVERT(100, "ft","m"),"ft","m")	Converting 100 square feet to square meters	9.290304

4.3 DEC2BIN

Dec2Bin converts decimal to binary. The syntax:

DEC2BIN(number, [position])

See pic below to convert decimal to binary:

	A	B	C
1			
2	DECIMAL		BINARY
3		144	10010000
4		124	1111100
5		123	1111011
6			
7			
8			
9			

Pic 4.3 Dec2Bin function

If number < -512 or >512 Dec2Bin function returns error #NUM!. If the number non-numeric, Dec2Bin will return error #VALUE.

See example below for more examples:

Formula	Description	Result
=DEC2BIN(9, 4)	Convert decimal 9 to binary 4 characters	1001
=DEC2BIN(-100)	Convert decimal -100 to binary.	1110011100

4.4 DEC2HEX

Dec2Hex function converts decimal to hexadecimal. Some notes about this function:

If number < -549,755,813,888 or > 549,755,813,887, function returns error #NUM!.

If value inserted non-numeric, function returns #VALUE!.

The second argument is character count. This can be used as padding by adding trailing 0 in front of the number.

If the second argument deleted, the function will use minimum amount to display character.

If the second argument is non-numeric, this will return error #VALUE!. If it is negative, will return error #NUM!.

	A	B	C	D	E	F
1						
2						
3		Dec	Hex			
4		12	C			
5		134	86			
6		141	8D			
7		123	7B			
8						
9						
10						
11						
12						
13						

Pic 4.4 Dec2Hex function

See table below for Dec2Hex examples:

Formula	Description	Result

=DEC2HEX (100, 4)	Converting decimal value 100 to 4 characters' hexadecimal	0064
=DEC2HEX (-54)	Converting -54 decimal to hexadecimal	FFFFFFFFCA

4.5 DELTA

Delta function tests whether the two values are the same. This will return 1 if number1= number2, If not, returns 0. You can use this function for filtering value.

This function also called Kronecker Delta. The syntax:

DELTA(number1, [number2])

Arguments

- ⊕ **Number1,** first number.

- ⊕ **Number2,** optional. The second number, if deleted, it is assumed = 0.

Notes:

- ⊕ If number1 = non-numeric, DELTA function returns #VALUE! error.

- ⊕ If number2 = non-numeric, DELTA function returns #VALUE! error.

Pic 4.5 Delta function

See table below for DELTA function examples:

Formula	Description	Result
=DELTA(5, 4)	Checking whether 5 = 4	0
=DELTA(5, 5)	Checking whether 5 = 5	1
=DELTA(0.5, 0)	Checking whether 0.5 = s0	0

4.6   GESTEP

The gestep function returns 1 if number tested ≥ step. Or if false, returns 0. The syntax:

GESTEP(number, [step])

Arguments:

⊕   Number: mandatory, the value tested.

🕐   Step: Optional, if empty, getstep will use zero.

If argument non-numeric, getstep will return #VALUE! Error.

Pic 4.6 Gestep function

See table below for more examples:

Formula	Description	Result
=GESTEP(5, 4)	Check whether 5 >= 4	1
=GESTEP(5, 5)	Check whether 5 >= 5	1
=GESTEP(-4, -5)	Check whether -4 >= -5	1
=GESTEP(-1, 0)	Check whether -1 >= 0	0

4.7   HEX2DEC

Hex2Dec will convert hexadecimal value to decimal. If not available in your Excel, you should load add-in in Analysis ToolPak.

You cannot enter more than 10 chars (40bit). If argument not hexadecimal, the HEX2DEC function returns #NUM! error.

C4			▼		×	✓	*fx*		=HEX2DEC(B4)	

⊿	A	B	C	D	E	F
1						
2						
3		HEX	DEC			
4		2	2			
5		3A	58			
6		12F	303			
7		1B	27			
8						
9						

Pic 4.7 Hex2Dec function

See table below for Hex2Dec function in Excel:

Formula	Description	Result
=HEX2DEC("FFFFFFFF5B")	Convert hex FFFFFFFF5B to decimal	-165
=HEX2DEC("3DA408B9")	Converting hex 3DA408B9 to decimal	1034160313

Excel supports financial calculation very well. Lots of functions available in excel related to financial needs.

5.1 DB

DB function returns depreciation of asset on certain period. The method used is fixed-declining. The syntax:

DB(price, balance, life, period, [month])

The arguments:

- ⊕ Cost, mandatory, the initial cost of the asset.
- ⊕ Salvage, mandatory, the value at the end of the depreciation (sometimes called the salvage value of the asset).
- ⊕ Life, mandatory, the number of periods over which the asset is being depreciated (sometimes called the useful life of the asset).
- ⊕ Period, mandatory, the period for which you want to calculate the depreciation. The period must use the same units as life.
- ⊕ Month, optional, the number of months in the first year. If the month is omitted, it is assumed to be 12.

For fixed-declining, DB use formula below to calculate depreciation for a period:

(price – total depreciation from previous period) * rate

Where:

rate = 1 - ((salvage/ price) ^ (1 / period)),

This is rounded to three decimal points.

First and last period using special formula. For the first period:

Price * rate * month / 12

For last period, DB uses this formula:

((price − total depreciation from previous period) * rate * (12 - month)) / 12

For example, see table below:

	A	B
1	Data	Description
2	1,000,000	Price
3	100,000	Salvage Value
4	6	Period (years)

You can create formula below:

Formula	Description	Result
=DB(A2,A3,A4,1,7)	Depreciation in the first year, only 7 months calculated.	186,083.33
=DB(A2,A3,A4,2,7)	Depreciation in the second year	259,639.42
=DB(A2,A3,A4,3,7)	Depreciation in the third year.	176,814.44

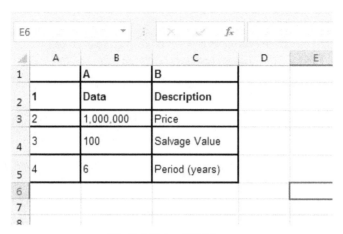

Pic 5.1 Using DB Menu

5.2   SLN

SLN function returns straight-line depreciation for an asset in one period:

SLN(price, salvage, period)

Pic 5.2 SLN function

For example, you can see data on the table below:

	A	B
1	Data	Description
2	30,000	Price
3	7,500	Salvage
4	10	Period

See table below for SLN function example using above data:

Formula	Description	Result
=SLN(A2, A3, A4)	Each year depreciation.	2,250

5.3   SYD

SYD function returns asset depreciation using the sum-of-years method on a certain period, the syntax:

SYD(price, salvage, life, period)

SYD function calculated using the function below:

$$SYD = \frac{(salvage\_value)*(life - period + 1)*2}{(life)(life + 1)}$$

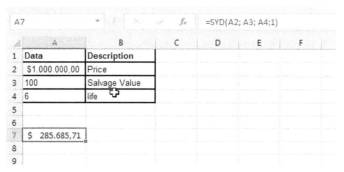

Pic 5.3 DB function

For example, data are shown here:

	A	B
1	Data	Description
2	30,000	Price
3	7,500	Salvage value
4	10	Life

You can see SYD examples in the table below:

Formula	Description	Result
=SYD(A2,A3,A4,1)	First-year depreciation	4,090.91
=SYD(A2,A3,A4,10)	10th-year annual depreciation	409.09

Information functions enable you to manage information in excel. Lots of information related functions will be described here.

6.1   CELL

CELL function returns formatting, location and content of the cell. For example, you can check or verify whether a cell content is numeric or not before using its content for arithmetical operations.

    =IF(CELL("type", A1) = "v", A1 * 2, 0)

This formula will calculate A1 *2 if only A1 has a numeric value. And will return 0 if A1 text or empty. The syntax:

    CELL(info_type, [reference])

About the arguments:

- ⊕   Info_type: the type that defines information of the cell.

- ⊕   reference. The cell you want to find the information. If empty, the last information in info_type will be returned to the last cell of range.

Some arguments for info_type:

INFO_TYPE	Returns
"address"	Reference from the first cell in reference as text.

"col"	Column number in reference.
"color"	1 if the cell formatted in color for negative, if not, this will be zero.
"contents"	Value from top-left in reference and not the formula.
"filename"	Filename, including the path of the file. This will return empty text ("") if worksheet not saved.
"format"	Returns "-" at the end of texts if cell formatted for negative values. Returns "()" at the end of texts if cell formatted with brackets for positive values or all values.
"parentheses"	1 if cell formatted with brackets or all values, if not, will return 0.
"prefix"	Text value related to "prefix label" of the cell. Will return one quote (') if the cell has negative alignment, and double quote (") if the cell contains right alignment. Exponent sign (^) if the cell has centered alignment, backslash (\) if the cell has fill-aligned and empty texts ("") if the cell has others.
"protect"	0 if cell unlocked, if not will return 1 if locked.

"row"	Row value from a cell by reference.
"type"	Text value related to a data type in a cell. Will return "b" for blank if the cell is blank, "l" for the label if the cell contains text, and "v" for value if the cell contains other.
"width"	The column width of a cell, rounded to an integer. The width of one column will be the width of one character in a standard font.

The table below shows the returned values of CELL function when info_type = "format" and reference is cell formatted with a built-in format.

If Excel Format	Returns
General	"G"
0	"F0"
#,##0	",0"
0.00	"F2"
#,##0.00	",2"
$#,##0_);($#,##0)	"C0"
$#,##0_);[Red]($#,##0)	"C0-"
$#,##0.00_);($#,##0.00)	"C2"

$#,##0.00_);[Red]($#,##0.00)	"C2-"
0%	"P0"
0.00%	"P2"
0.00E+00	"S2"
# ?/? atau # ??/??	"G"
m/d/yy atau m/d/yy h:mm atau mm/dd/yy	"D4"
d-mmm-yy atau dd-mmm-yy	"D1"
d-mmm atau dd-mmm	"D2"
mmm-yy	"D3"
mm/dd	"D5"
h:mm AM/PM	"D7"
h:mm:ss AM/PM	"D6"
h:mm	"D9"
h:mm:ss	"D8"

C2	▼	:	×	✓	ƒx	=CELL("contents";B2)

	A	B	C	D	E	F	G	H
1								
2		24/01/2015	42028					
3		Rp10.000	10000					
4		9800,98	9800,98					
5								
6								
7								
8								
9								
10								

Pic 6.1 CELL function

For example, here is the content of range A1:C2:

	A	B	C
1	**Data**		
2	**5-Mar**		

See table below for cell function examples:

Formula	Description	Result
=CELL("row", A20)	Row number for A20	20
=CELL("format", A2)	Format code for A2	D2 (d-mmm)
=CELL("type", A2)	Data type for A2	v (value)

6.2 COUNTBLANK

Counting blank cell on ranges. The syntax is:

COUNTBLANK(range)

A cell with a formula that returns the blank text "" also calculated. Cell with value = 0 (zero) is not calculated.

Pic 6.2 COUNTBLANK function

For example, you can see the condition of range A1: B5 on this table:

	A	B
1	Data	Data
2		
3	6	=IF(B4<30,"",B4)
4		27
5	4	34

See table below for COUNTBLANK function example:

Formula	Description	Result
=COUNTBLANK(A2:B5)	Return blank cell A2:B5. Where formula on B3 returns an empty value.	4

6.3   ERROR.TYPE

Error.Type function returns error number from error in excel. Or will return #N/A if there is no error happened. The syntax is:

ERROR.TYPE(error_number)

Here is some type of errors the function can return:

If Error	ERROR.TYPE returns
#NULL!	1
#DIV/0!	2
#VALUE!	3
#REF!	4
#NAME?	5
#NUM!	6

#N/A	7
#GETTING_DATA	8
other	#N/A

For example, in range A1: B3:

	A	**B**
1	**Data**	
2	#NULL!	
3	=1/0	

See table below for Error.type function example:

Formula	**Description**	**Result**
=ERROR.TYPE(A2)	The number for #NULL! Error	1

6.4   INFO

Returns information about operating environment. The syntax is:

INFO(type_text)

Type_text details:

TYPE_TEXT	**Returns**

"directory"	The path from working directory or folder.
"numfile"	Active worksheet in opened workbook.
"origin"	Absolute cell reference. This depends on reference style you use. For example, using D9 as main reference, you can return: • **A1 style reference** "$A:$D$9". • **R1C1 style reference**"$A:R9C4"
"osversion"	Operating system version, as text.
"recalc"	Recalculation method, returns "Automatic" or "Manual".
"release"	The version of Microsoft Excel, as text.
"system"	Name of operating system, for Macintosh = "mac" for Windows = "pcdos"

See table below for INFO function examples:

Formula	Description	Result
=INFO("numfile")	Amount of Active worksheet	Varies

=INFO("recalc")	Recalculating method for workbook	Automatic or Manual

Pic 6.3 INFO function in Excel

6.5   ISBLANK

ISBLANK function returns TRUE if cell = blank, and FALSE if not blank. The syntax is:

ISBLANK (value)

Value tested can be an empty cell, error expressions, text, number, reference value, or reference to components.

Pic 6.4 ISBLANK function

See table below for ISBLANK function examples, where A2 = , and cell A3 is empty.

Formula	Description	Result
=ISBLANK (A2)	Check whether A2 cell = empty	FALSE
=ISBLANK (A3)	Check whether A3 = empty.	TRUE

6.6   ISERR

ISERR function returns TRUE if error value exists, excluding #N/A; if not will return FALSE.

The syntax:

iserr (value)

Value tested can be an empty cell, a logical expression, text, number, reference number, or reference cell.

Pic 6.5 ISERR function

The argument should be closed with double quote and cannot be converted to another type. For example, you can see data below:

	A
1	**Data**
2	**#REF!**
3	**#N/A**

See table below for other ISERR example:

Formula	Description	Result
=ISERR (A2)	Checks whether the A2 error is not #N/A.	TRUE
=ISERR (A3)	Checks whether the A3 error is not #N/A.	FALSE

6.7   ISERROR

ISERROR function checks whether the error exists, then returns TRUE or FALSE. This can be used to in formula.

C2	▼		fx	=A2/B2					
	A	B	C	D	E	F	G	H	I
1	829	2	414.5						
2	953	0	#DIV/0!						
3	946	4	236.5						
4	604	4	151						
5	576	3	192						
6	554	5	110.8						
7	637	0	#DIV/0!						
8	560	2	280						
9	672	4	168						
10	728	10	72.8						
11									
12									

Pic 6.6 IsError function

You can combine IF and ISERROR so if the error exists, a certain number will be displayed, and the Error code will not appear.

C2	▼	fx	=IF(ISERROR(A2/B2),5,100)						
	A	B	C	D	E	F	G	H	I
1	829	2	100						
2	953	0	5						
3	946	4	100						
4	604	4	100						
5	576	3	100						
6	554	5	100						
7	637	0	5						
8	560	2	100						
9	672	4	100						
10	728	10	100						
11									
12									

Pic 6.7 Combining IF and ISERROR

6.8   ISEVEN

ISEVEN function returns TRUE if number evens, and FALSE if number odds. If this function unavailable, and returns #NAME?, you must install and load Analysis ToolPak add-in.

The syntax is:

ISEVEN(number)

See image below:

C4			▼ ⋮ ✕ ✓	fx	=ISEVEN(B4)	
	A	B	C	D	E	F
1		Data	ISEVEN			
2		5	FALSE			
3		1	FALSE			
4		2,5	TRUE			
5						
6						
7						

Pic 6.8 ISEVEN function

If number = non-numeric, ISEVEN will returns #VALUE! error.

See table below for ISEVEN function examples:

Formula	Description	Result
=ISEVEN(-1)	Checks whether -1 is even number	FALSE
=ISEVEN(2.5)	Checks whether 2.5 is even number	TRUE
=ISEVEN(5)	Checks whether 5 is an even number.	FALSE

6.9   ISLOGICAL

ISLOGICAL function checks whether certain value = logical value (TRUE or FALSE) or not.

ISLOGICAL(value)

If the value = logical value, this function returns TRUE, if not, will return FALSE.

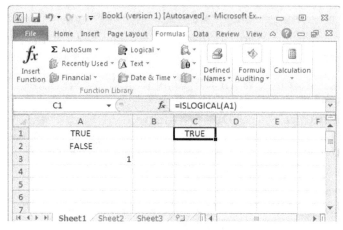

Pic 6.9 Data in range A1:A3

See table below for ISLOGICAL function examples:

Formula	Description	Result
=ISLOGICAL(A1)	Checking whether A1 = logical value	TRUE
=ISLOGICAL(A2)	Checking whether A2 = logical value	TRUE
=ISLOGICAL(TRUE)	Checking whether TRUE value = logical	TRUE
=ISLOGICAL("TRUE")	Checking whether string "TRUE" = logical value.	FALSE

6.10 ISNA

ISNA function returns TRUE if error = #N/A (value not available), if not will return FALSE.

The syntax:

ISNA(value)

The value argument can be empty cell, error, logical expression, text, or reference to another cell.

C3			▼	⋮	✕	✓	*fx*	=ISNA(B3)

	A	B	C	D	E	F
1		ERROR	CEK			
2		1/0	FALSE			
3		#N/A	TRUE			
4						
5						
6						
7						

Pic 6.10 ISNA function

For example, data from A1:A5 like this:

	A
1	**Data**
2	#REF!
3	#N/A
4	#NUM!
5	#DIV/0

See table below for ISNA function examples:

Formula	Description	Result
=ISNA (A2)	Checking whether error in A2 = #N/A	FALSE
=ISNA (A3)	Checking whether error in A3 = #N/A	TRUE

6.11 ISNONTEXT

ISNONTEXT function returns TRUE if value = non text, and returns FALSE if value = text. The syntax:

ISNONTEXT(value)

If value inserted = non-text or blank, ISNONTEXT value will return TRUE. An empty string = considered text.

See table below for ISNONTEXT function examples:

Formula	Description	Result
=ISNONTEXT (7)	Checking whether 7 = non-text value.	TRUE
=ISNONTEXT ("7")	Checking whether "7" non-text value.	FALSE

6.12 ISNUMBER

ISNUMBER function checks whether value = number or not a number. The syntax is:

ISNUMBER(value)

See example below:

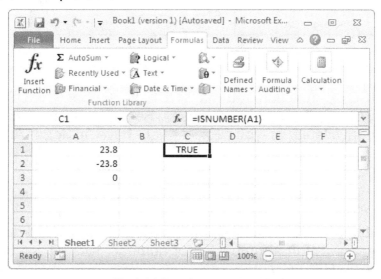

Pic 6.11 Data in range A1:A3

See table below for ISNUMBER function examples:

Formula	Description	Result
=ISNUMBER(A1)	Checking whether A1 = number.	TRUE
=ISNUMBER(A2)	Checking whether A2 = number.	TRUE

=ISNUMBER(A3)	Checking whether A3 = number.	TRUE
=ISNUMBER(5)	Checking whether 5 = number	TRUE
=ISNUMBER("5")	Checking whether string "5" = number.	FALSE

6.13 ISODD

ISODD function returns TRUE if number = ODD, and FALSE if number = even. FALSE. If this function unavailable in your Excel, you have to load Analysis ToolPak add-in first.

The syntax is:

ISODD(number)

If the number is not an integer, it will be rounded down to integer. If the number = not numeric, ISODD will display #VALUE! error.

▲	A	B	C	D
1	VALUE	ISODD		
2	$ 10.00	FALSE		
3	11.5	TRUE		
4	1	TRUE		
5				
6				
7				

Pic 6.12 ISODD function

See table below for more ISODD function examples:

Formula	Description	Result
=ISODD(-1)	Checking whether -1 = odd	TRUE
=ISODD(2.5)	Checking whether 2.5 = odd.	FALSE
=ISODD(5)	Checking whether 5 = odd	TRUE

6.14 ISREF

ISREF function is for checking the reference. The syntax is:

ISREF(value)

If the value is the reference, the ISREF function returns TRUE, if not, return FALSE. See pic below, where B1= A1 + A2 + A3:

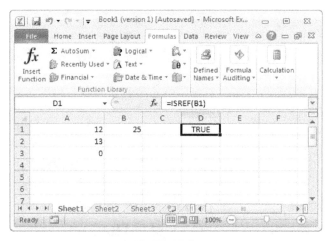

Pic 6.13 ISREF function

See table below for more ISREF function examples:

Formula	Description	Result
=ISREF(B1)	Checking whether B1 cell is the reference or not.	TRUE
=ISREF(A1+A2)	Checking whether A1 + A2 is the reference or not.	FALSE

6.15 ISTEXT

ISTEXT function is for checking whether value = text or not. The syntax is:

ISTEXT(value)

If Value = Text, this function will return True, if not will return false. See pic below:

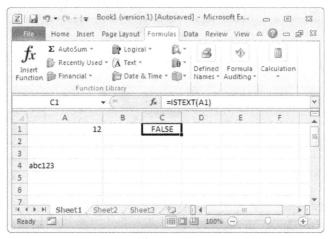

Pic 6.14 ISTEXT function

Here are some examples of ISTEXT function:

Formula	Description	Result

=ISTEXT(A1)	Checking whether A1 = text or not	FALSE
=ISTEXT(A3)	Checking whether A3 = text or not.	FALSE
=ISTEXT(A4)	Checking whether A4 = text or not.	TRUE
=ISTEXT("testExcel")	Checking whether string "testExcel" = text or not	TRUE

6.16 N

N function returns value converted to a number.

N(value)

Value is the value you want to convert. See table below:

If Value refer to	N returns
Number	The number
Date	Date in Serial number
TRUE	1
FALSE	0
Error value, for example, #DIV/0!	The error value

Others	0

For example, data in A1:A5:

	A
1	Data
2	7
3	Even
4	TRUE
5	4/17/2014

See table below for N function examples:

Formula	Description	Result
=N(A2)	Because A2 = number, the number returned.	7
=N(A3)	Because A3 = text, 0 will be returned.	0
=N(A4)	Because A4 = logical value TRUE, 1 will be returned.	1

6.17 NA

NA function returns #N/A error. #N/A means not available. You can generate #NA on an empty cell, for certain reasons, for example, to avoid inserting data to certain cells. The syntax is:

NA( )

NA function does not need arguments

Pic 6.15 NA function

Logic functions process Boolean values. Boolean only has two values, TRUE or FALSE. But can be used extensively to manage the flow of formulas in excel.

7.1   AND

AND function returns TRUE if all the arguments = TRUE and return FALSE if, one or more arguments = FALSE.

The syntax is:

AND(logic_value1, [logic_value2], ...)

Logic_value1 is mandatory, it is the first condition to test using AND. The value can be TRUE or FALSE.

Logic_value2, optional. This is an additional value; you can add up to 255 conditions. See pic below:

J12				fx		
	A	B	C	D	E	F
1						
2						
3		Val1	Val2	AND		
4		TRUE	TRUE	TRUE		
5		FALSE	TRUE	FALSE		
6		FALSE	TRUE	FALSE		
7		FALSE	FALSE	FALSE		
8						
9						
10						

Pic 7.1 Fungsi AND to BOOLEAN operator

See table below for more AND function examples:

Formula	Description	Result
=AND(TRUE, TRUE)	All arguments = TRUE	TRUE
=AND(TRUE, FALSE)	One of arguments = FALSE	FALSE
=AND(2+2=4, 2+3=5)	All arguments = TRUE	TRUE

For example, data in range A1:A3 like this:

	A
1	Data
2	50
3	104

See table below for AND function examples:

Formula	Description	Result
=AND(1<A2, A2<100)	Display TRUE if 1 < A2 <100. If not, will display false.	TRUE
=IF(AND(1<A3, A3<100), A3, "Out of range.")	Display the value in A3, if the value between 1 and 100. If not, it will display a string text.	Out of range

=IF(AND(1<A2, A2<100), A2, "Out of range.")	Displaying the content of A2 if the value between 1 and 100, if not, will display a string text.	50

7.2   IF

IF function returns value based on condition or returns other if the condition not met. For example:

=IF(A1>10,"more than 10","10 or less")

The code displays "more than 10" if the value of A1 > 10, or displays the second texts if the value of A1 not > 10.

The syntax for IF statement:

If(logical_test, [if_true], [if_false])

Notes:

- Logical_test: mandatory, this is a value or expression that can be valued as TRUE or FALSE. For example, A1 = 100, this expression is a logical expression. If the content of cell A1 = 100, it will be true, if not, it will be False.

- If_true: optional, value returned if logical_test = True.

- if_false, optional, value returned if logical_test = False.

You can add up to 64 nested ifs, but this is rarely used because the codes will be hard to read. If logical_test enormous, you can use other functions instead, such as: LOOKUP, VLOOKUP, HLOOKUP, or CHOOSE.

For example, you can see data in A1:A2 like this:

	A
1	Data
2	50

See table below for more IF statement examples:

Formula	Description	Result
=IF(A2<=100,"Below budget","Above budget")	If value in A2 <= 100, the text "Below budget" shown, if not, "Above budget" shown.	"Below budget"
=IF(A2=100,A2+B2,"")	If A2 = 100, then will display sum of A2 + B2. If not, will display empty string	Empty string

7.3   NOT

NOT function returns inverse of argument value. The syntax is:

NOT(logical_value)

logical_value is a value or expression that can be valued as TRUE or FALSE. If logical_value = FALSE, NOT function will return TRUE, if logical_value = TRUE, NOT function will return FALSE.

Pic 7.2 NOT function

See table below for more NOT function examples:

Formula	Description	Result
=NOT(FALSE)	Returns FALSE	TRUE
=NOT(1+1=2)	The equation = TRUE, so the function returns false	FALSE

7.4 OR

OR function returns TRUE if at least one of arguments has TRUE value. And will return FALSE, if all arguments = FALSE.

The syntax:

OR(logical_value1,logical_value2,...)

You can use logical_values up to 255.

▲	A	B	C	D	E	F	G
1							
2							
3		Val1	Val2	OR			
4		TRUE	TRUE	TRUE			
5		FALSE	TRUE	TRUE			
6		FALSE	TRUE	TRUE			
7		FALSE	FALSE	FALSE			
8							
9							
10							
11							
12							

Pic 7.3 OR function

See table below for or function examples:

Formula	Description (Result)	Result
=OR(TRUE)	One argument TRUE	TRUE
=OR(1+1=1,2+2=5)	All Arguments = FALSE	FALSE

=OR(TRUE,FALSE,TRUE)	At least one argument = TRUE	TRUE

Lookup used when lots of alternatives exist, usually in array or range. Excel supports various lookup functions.

8.1   CHOOSE

Fungsi CHOOSE use index_num function to choose value from arguments. You can use CHOOSE to choose 1 up to 254 values based on index number.

For example, 1 - 7 is day in a week. CHOOSE function will return one value between 1 and 7 using index_number. The syntax is:

CHOOSE(index_number, value1, value2, ...)

Index_number define the selected argument. This number should be between 1 and 254, or also can be formula, or reference to cell that contain number between 1 and 254.

If index_number = 1, CHOOSE function will choose value1, if index_number 2, CHOOSE will choose value2, etc.

If index_number less than 1, or more than last number, CHOOSE function will return #VALUE! error. If index_number = not integer/real number, will be rounded down to closest integer before used.

Argument can be from 1 to 254. Arguments can be number, cell reference, name, formula, function, or texts.

If index_number = array, all values will be evaluated when CHOOSE evaluated. Value argument is being selected with CHOOSE can be range reference, or single value. For example, this formula:

=SUM(CHOOSE(2,A1:A10,B1:B10,C1:C10))

Is the same with:

=SUM(B1:B10)

This will return value in range B1:B10.

Pic 8.1 CHOOSE function

For example, you can see data below in range A1:B5:

	A	B
1	Data	Data
2	1st	Arrow
3	2nd	Ice
4	3rd	Brake

5	4rd	Strawberry

See table below for CHOOSE function examples:

Formula	Description	Result
=CHOOSE(2,A2,A3,A4,A5)	Value from argument (2nd)	2nd
=CHOOSE(4,B2,B3,B4,B5)	Value for 4th argument in cell B5	Strawberry

8.2   HLOOKUP

HLOOKUP function will do horizontal lookup. Syntax for HLOOKUP function like this:

HLOOKUP(value, table, index_number, [if_not_precise])

Argument details:

- Value: This is the value of the first line of the table.

- Table: two or more rows sorted on ascending order.

- Index_number: row number in table where suitable value will be returned. First row =1.

- If_not_precise: This is optional, if you want precise result, you can enter FALSE. For approaching method, you can enter TRUE.

Some notes:

- If index_number more than one, HLOOKUP will return #VALUE! error.

⊕ If index_number more than column count in table, HLOOKUP returns #REF!

⊕ If you enter FALSE for parameter, if not precise, HLOOKUP function returns #N/A value.

See data below in range A1:C4

	A	B	C
1	Axle	Bearing	Bolt
2	4	4	9
3	5	7	10
4	6	8	11

	A	B	C	D
1	Axle	Bearing	Bolt	
2	4	4	9	
3	5	7	10	
4	6	8	11	
5				
6				
7				
8				
9				

Pic 8.2 HLOOKUP function

Look data below to see HLOOKUP function examples:

Formula	Description	Result
=HLOOKUP(" Axle",A1:C4,2 ,TRUE)	Finding "Axle" in first row, and then returning value from second row in the same column.	4

=HLOOKUP(" Bearing",A1: C4,3,FALSE)	Find "Bearing" in first row, and return value from third row in the same column.	7

8.3 INDEX

Index function will return value or reference to table or range. There are two types of INDEX function, array form and reference form.

Array Form returns value from element into able or array. It is selected based on row and column index.

Use array form if first argument of INDEX = Array constant.

The syntax is:

INDEX(array,row_num,column_num)

Argument details:

- ⏀ Array: range or array constant. If array have one row and one column, only row_num and column_num used, INDEX function returns array from all rows or columns.

- ⏀ Row_num: row in array that will return value. If this is empty, column_num is mandatory.

- ⏀ Column_num: column in array that will return value. If column_num empty, row_num is mandatory.

If you enter row_num and column_num. INDEX function will return value in intersection between intersection of row_num and column_num.

If you set row_num or column_num = 0, INDEX function will use value array from all rows and columns.

To enter array formula, click CTRL+SHIFT+ENTER. Row_num and column_num have to be cell in array, if not, INDEX will return #REF! error.

For example, see data in range A1:B3:

	A	B
1	**Data**	**Data**
2	Apple	Orange
3	Pineapple	Pear

See table below for index function examples:

Formula	**Description**	**Result**
=INDEX(A2: B3,2,2)	Value in intersection between second row and second column.	Pear
=INDEX(A2: B3,2,1)	Value in intersection between second row and first column in range.	Pineapp le

Form reference returns reference of intersection cell from row and column. The syntax:

INDEX(reference,row_num,column_num, area_num)

For example, content of range A1:C11 looks like this:

	A	B	C
1	Fruit	Price	Jumlah
2	Apple	0.69	40
3	Lemon	0.34	38
4	Banana	0.55	15
5	Orange	0.25	25
6	Pear	0.59	40
7			
8	Almond	2.80	10
9	Cashew	3.55	16
10	Nuts	1.25	20
11	Pineapple	1.75	12

See table below for Index function examples:

Formula	Description	Result
=INDEX(A2:C6,2,3)	Intersection between 2nd row and 1st column in range A2:C6, that is the	38

	content of C3 cell.	
=INDEX((A1:C6,A8:C11),2,2,2)	Intersection between 2nd row and 2nd column in A8:C11, this is the content of B9.	3,55

8.4   INDIRECT

INDIRECT functino returns reference by text strings. The syntax is:

INDIRECT(ref_text,a1)

Arguments details:

- ⊕ Ref_text: reference to cell.
- ⊕ A1 logical value that deterimne reference in ref_text cell. If a1 = TRUE or empty, ref_text interpreted as A1-style reference. If A1 = FALSE, ref_text interpreted as R1C1-style reference.

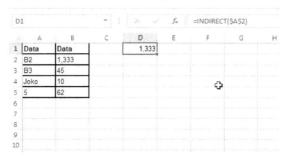

Pic 8.4 Indirect function

For example, data in range A1:B5:

	A	B
1	Data	Data
2	B2	1.333
3	B3	45
4	Joko	10
5	5	62

See table below for INDIRECT function examples:

Formula	Description	Result
=INDIRECT($A$2)	Value for reference in A2	1.333
=INDIRECT($A$3)	Value for reference in A3	45
=INDIRECT($A$4)	In A4 you can see "Joko," this defined number will be returned	10
=INDIRECT("B"&$A$5)	Value for reference in A5	62

8.5   LOOKUP (ARRAY)

Lookup array finds value in first row or column of array and then returns value from the last row or column.

You can use this kind of lookup if value matched in first column or row. Lookup array almost similar with HLOOKUP or VLOOKUP. HLOOKUP finds value in first row, VLOOKUP finds value in first column, while LOOKUP finds according to array dimension.

Actually, using VLOOKUP or HLOOKUP is better than using LOOKUP. This function available for the sake of compatibility with other spreadsheet program. The syntax is:

LOOKUP(lookup_value,array)

Using the same data used in INDIRECT function above, see table below for LOOKUP function examples:

Formula	Description	Result
=LOOKUP ("C",{"a","b ","c","d";1, 2,3,4})	Find "C" in first row, and returns value in last row in the same column.	3
=LOOKUP ("joko",{"a", 1;"b",2;"c", 3})	Find text "joko" in first row of array and returns value in the last column in the same row,	2

8.6 LOOKUP (VECTOR)

Second lookup function has the same function, but not in array. The syntax is:

LOOKUP(value, range_lookup, [range_Result])

If LOOKUP cant find precise data, it will choose the largest value in range_lookup that is equal or smaller than the value.

See data below:

	A	B	C	D	E	F
1	ID Order	Product	Price	Qty		
2	10247	Apple	14	12		
3	10249	Orange	9.8	10		
4	10250	Banana	34.8	5		
5	10251	Pear	18.6	9		
6	10252	Grape	42.3	40		
7						
8						
9						

Pic 8.5 Data for LOOKUP function

See table below for LOOKUP function examples:

For mula	Description	Result
=LOOKUP(10251 , A1:A6)	Find 10251 in the first column.	10251
=LOOKUP(10246 , A1:A6, B1:B6)	Find 10246 in the first column but not available	#N/A

8.7 MATCH

Match function finds the position in range. For example, if range A1:A3 have values 5, 25, and 38, then the formula below:

=MATCH(25,A1:A3,0)

Will return 2, because 25 is the 2nd item in the range.

The syntax is:

MATCH(lookup_value, lookup_array, [match_type])

For match_type, you can have these values:

Match Type	Description
1 or empty	MATCH finds largest value that is less or equal with lookup_value. Values in lookup_array have to be in ascending order, eg:...-2, -1, 0, 1, 2, ..., A-Z, FALSE, TRUE.
0	MATCH finds first value that is exactly the same with lookup_value. Values in lookup_array can have ascending or descending order.
-1	MATCH finds smallest value that is larger or equal with lookup_value. Values in lookup_array sorted in descending order.eg: TRUE, FALSE, Z-A, ...2, 1, 0, -1, -2, ..., etc.

Some notes:

- ⊕ **MATCH** returns matched value's position in lookup_array, not the value itself, for example, **MATCH("b",{"a","b","c"},0)** will return 2, that is the relative position "b" inside array {"a","b","c"}.

- ⊕ **MATCH** function doesn't distinguish between uppercase and lowercase when matching texts.

- ⊕ If **MATCH** cannot matching values, it will display error #N/A.

For example, data in range A1 : B6 in the table below:

	A	**B**
1	**Product**	**Amount**
2	Pineapple	25
3	Orange	38
4	Apple	40
5	Pear	41

See table below for Match function examples:

Formula	Description	Result
=MATCH (39,B2:B 5,1)	Because there is no matched result, returns the lowest position in B2:B5	2

=MATCH (41,B2:B 5,0)	The position of 41 in range B2:B5.	4
=MATCH (40,B2:B 5,-1)	Returns error because values in B2:B5 not in descending order.	#N/A

8.8   SUM DENGAN OFFSET

Pic 8.6 SUM with offset

The syntax of OFFSET function:

= OFFSET (reference, row, column, height, width)

Arguments details:

- Reference: start point for the function. You can reference cell from offset calculation, you can define how much rows and columns count. Reference argument can refer to a single cell or adjacent cells.

- Row: mandatory, rows count below or above reference argument, used to calculate offset. This value can be positive, negative or zero.

🕐 Column: columns count int the left or right reference argument. This value can be positive, negative or zero.

🕐 Height: optional, setting height from returned offset. This value has to be positive.

🕐 Width: optional, setting width from returned offset. This value has to be positive.

8.9 TRANSPOSE

TRANSPOSE function returns a vertical range of cells as horizontal range and vice versa, Here's the syntax:

TRANSPOSE(array)

Pic 8.7 TRANSPOSE function

For example, you can see data below in range A1:C2:

	A	B	C
1	Data	Data	Data
2	1	2	3

From above data, see table below for transpose

Formula	Description	Result
=TRANSPOSE($A$2:$C$2)	Value from 1st column	1
	Value from 2nd column	2
	Value from 3rd column	3

When creating transpose, set cells, and then click CTRL + SHIFT + ENTER to insert values.

8.10 VLOOKUP

The vlookup function looks like HLOOKUP, but the searching is vertical. The syntax is:

VLOOKUP(lookup_value,   table_array,   column_index_number, [lookup_range])

	A	B	C	D	E
1	Density	Viscosity	Temperature	VLOOKUP	
2	0,457	3,55	500	2,17	
3	0,525	3,25	400		
4	0,606	2,93	300		
5	0,675	2,75	250		
6	0,746	2,57	200		
7	0,835	2,38	150		
8	0,946	2,17	100		
9	1,09	1,95	50		
10	1,29	1,71	0		
11					

Pic 8.8 VLOOKUP function example

For example, data in range A1:C10:

	A	B	C

1	Density	Viscosity	Temp
2	0,457	3,55	500
3	0,525	3,25	400
4	0,606	2,93	300
5	0,675	2,75	250
6	0,746	2,57	200
7	0,835	2,38	150
8	0,946	2,17	100
9	1,09	1,95	50
10	1,29	1,71	0

See table below for VLOOKUP function examples:

Formula	Description	Result
=VLOOKUP (1,A2:C10,2)	Finding value near 1 in column A, Finding largest value <= 1 in A column, that is .946, then find another value from B column in the same row.	2,17
=VLOOKUP (0.7,A2:C10 ,3,FALSE)	Using exact method, finding 0.7 in column A,	#N/A

	because not found, will returns error	

Statistics operations supported by excel. Excel have lots of functions related to statistics. This chapter describes most important excel functions in statistics.

9.1 AVERAGE

The average function returns arithmetical mean from data. The syntax:

AVERAGE(number1, [number2],...)

- ⊕ The first argument is mandatory, it has to be a number, cell reference or range.

- ⊕ Number2 optional. You can add up to 255 number.

Arguments details:

- ⊕ All arguments have to be numeric.

- ⊕ If range's or cell's content = text, logical value or empty cell, the value will not be considered.

- ⊕ Error value arguments or text that cannot be casted as a number, will create ERROR in AVERAGE function..

For example, data in A1:C6 looks like this:

	A	B	C
1	Data		

2	10	15	32
3	7		
4	9		
5	27		
6	2		

See table below for more Average function examples:

Formula	Description	Result
=AVERAGE(A2:A6)	Average of range A2:A6.	11
=AVERAGE(A2:A6, 5)	Average of range A2:A6 plus 5	10
=AVERAGE(A2:C2)	Average of range A2:C2.	19

9.2 CORREL

CORREL function returns correlation coefficient from range array1 and array2. Correlation coefficient defines the connection between two data.

The syntax is:

CORREL(array1, array2)

If array1 and array2 have different amount of data, CORREL function will return error #N/A.

If array1 or array2 empty, s (deviation standard) and the value = zero, this will make CORREL function returns an error.

Because CORREL function calculated as below:

$$Correl(X,Y) = \frac{\sum (x - \bar{x})(y - \bar{y})}{\sqrt{\sum (x - \bar{x})^2 \sum (y - \bar{y})^2}}$$

Where $\bar{x}$ and $\bar{y}$ the mean of array 1/AVERAGE(array1) and mean of array 2/AVERAGE(array2).

	A	B	C	D	E
1	Data1	Data2	0,997054		
2	3	9			
3	2	7			
4	4	12			
5	5	15			
6	6	17			
7					
8					

Pic 9.1 CORREL function to calculate correlation

You can see data below:

	A	B
1	Data1	Data2
2	3	9
3	2	7
4	4	12

| 6 | 5 | 15 |
| 6 | 6 | 17 |

See table below for calculate example:

Formula	Description	Result
=CORREL(A2:A6,B2:B6)	Correlation coefficient from 2 data set.	0.997054

9.3   COUNT

COUNT function calculates amount of cells that contains a number and counting number of arguments. You can use COUNT to get the total number in ranges. For example, you can use a number in range A1:A20:

    =COUNT(A1:A20)

The syntax is:

    COUNT(value1, [value2], ...)

- ⏰ Value1: mandatory, first item, cell reference or range.

- ⏰ Value2: optional, you can add up to 255 items.

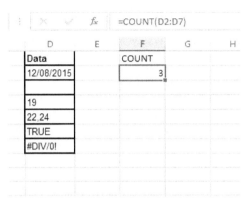

Pic 9.2 COUNT function

For example, data in range A1:A7:

	A
1	**Data**
2	12/8/015
3	
4	19
5	22,24
6	TRUE
7	#DIV/0!

From data above, see table below for COUNT function examples:

Formula	Description	Result

=COUNT(A2:A7)	Counting cells that have numeric content in A2:A7	3
=COUNT(A5:A7)	Counting cell that has numeric content between A5 and A7.	2
=COUNT(A2:A7,2)	Counting cell that has numeric content between A2 and A7, and value 2	4

9.4   COUNTA

COUNTA counts cells in a range that is not empty.

COUNTA(value1, [value2], ...)

COUNTA function counts all cells that have information, including error, and empty text.

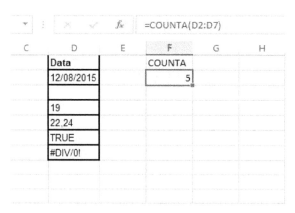

Pic 9.3 COUNTA function

For example, data in cell A1: A7:

	A
1	**Data**
2	Sales
3	12/8/2015
4	
5	19
6	22.24
7	TRUE
8	#DIV/0!

See table below for COUNTA function example:

Formula	Description	Result
=COUNTA(A2:A8)	Counting cells that don't have empty contents.	6

9.5   FORECAST

Forecast function forecasts or predicts future value based on existing data. The predicted value is Y, for specific X value.

The syntax is:

FORECAST(x, y_knowns, x_knowns)

X argument is mandatory. If x = not numeric, FORECAST will return error #VALUE!. If x_known and y_known empty or contains different data set, FORECAST function will return #N/A error.

If the variance of x_knowns = 0, Forecast function will return #DIV/0! error. For example,

	A	B
1	Y_known	X_known
2	6	20
3	7	28
4	9	31

| 5 | 15 | 38 |
| 6 | 21 | 40 |

See table below for FORECAST function example:

Formula	Description	Result
=FORECAST(30,A2:A6,B2:B6)	Predicts y value for x 30 value	10.60725

9.6   FREQUENCY

FREQUENCY function returns frequency of value in the range, then returns a vertical array of value.

Because FREQUENCY returns array, have to be entered as an array formula. The syntax is:

FREQUENCY(data_array, bins_array)

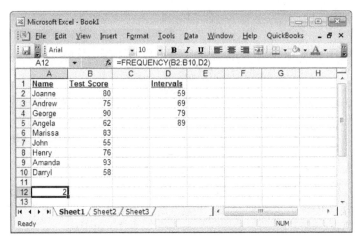

Pic 9.Frequency function

From data above, see table below for FREQUENCY function example:

Formula	Description	Result
=FREQUENCY(B2:B10,D2)	Calculating frequency B2:B10 with bins_array in D2	2
=FREQUENCY(B2:B10,D3)	Calculating frequency B2:B10 with bins_array in D3	3

9.7 LARGE

LARGE function returns k-th largest value from dataset/array. By using the LARGE function, you can count 1st largest, 2nd largest, 3rd largest, and so forth.

The syntax is:

LARGE(array,k)

If array empty, large will return #NUM! error value.

If k ≤ 0 or k > array member, the LARGE function will return #NUM! error value. For example, data in range A1:B6:

	A	B
1	**Data**	**Data**
2	3	4
3	5	2
4	3	4
5	5	6
6	4	7

See table below for LARGE function examples:

Formula	Description	Result

=LARGE(A2:B6,3)	The third largest number in the range above.	5
=LARGE(A2:B6,7)	7th largest number from numbers above.	4

9.8   MAX

MAX function returns largest value from dataset/array. The syntax is:

MAX(num1,num2,...)

You can add up to 255 number.

If arguments not numeric, MAX will return 0.

For example, you can see data below in range A1:A6.

	A
1	**Data**
2	10
3	7
4	9
5	27
6	2

From above data, see table below for MAX function examples:

Formula	Description	Result
=MAX(A2:A6)	Largest value from data above	27
=MAX(A2:A6, 30)	Largest value from data, plus number = 30.	30

9.9 MEDIAN

The median function returns median value from a dataset. Median is the number in the middle of a dataset. The syntax is:

MEDIAN(num1, [num2], ...)

You can add numbers up to 255 numbers. Arguments can be number or array, or reference to a number.

For example, data in range A1:A7:

	A
1	Data
2	1
3	2
4	3

5	4
6	5
7	6

See table below for MEDIAN function examples:

Formula	Description	Result
=MEDIAN(A2:A6)	Median from first 5 numbers.	3
=MEDIAN(A2:A7)	Median from all numbers	3,5

9.10 MIN

MIN function is the inverse of MAX function. This function returns the smallest value from data. The syntax is:

MIN(num1,num2,...)

You can add numbers up to 255 numbers. If arguments not numeric, MIN function will return 0. An argument can be error value.

For example, data in range A1:A6:

	A
1	Data
2	10

3	7
4	9
5	27
6	2

See table below for MIN function examples:

Formula	Description	Result
=MIN(A2:A6)	Smallest value from the range above.	2
=MIN(A2:A6,0)	Smallest value from the range above plus number = 0.	0

9.11 MODE

MODE function will return the mode, that is the most value exists in data/array, the syntax is:

MODE(num1,[num2],...])

You can add up to 255 numbers. If dataset doesn't have duplicate values for MODE, MODE function will return #N/An error. For example, data in cell A1:A7:

	A
1	Data

2	5.6
3	4
4	4
5	3
6	2
7	4

See example below for MODE function example:

Formula	Description	Result
=MODE(A2:A7)	Mode from data above	4

9.12 PERMUT

PERMUT function returns permutation for an object that can be chosen from a dataset. The permutation is set or a subset of objects where the internal order is important.

A permutation is different from combination where the internal order is not important.

PERMUT(number, number_choosen)

Both arguments mandatory. Both arguments should be an integer, If number < number_choosen, PERMUT will return #NUM! error. Here's the formula for PERMUT function:

$$P_{k,n} = \frac{n!}{(n-k)!}$$

For example, you can see data below in range A1:B3:

	A	B
1	Data	Description
2	100	Objects count
3	3	Object count in each permutation

See table below for PERMUT function example:

Formula	Description	Result
=PERMUT(A2,A3)	Permutation for data above	970200

9.13 QUARTILE

QUARTILE function returns quartile or 1/4-th data. The syntax is:

QUARTILE(array,quart)

The array is the data to find the quartile, while quart is a number from 0 to 4. Where 0 = min, and 4 = max.

Quart	Returns
0	Min value
1	First quartile (percentile 25)

2	Median (percentile 50)
3	Third quartile (percentile 75)
4	Max value

For example, you can see data in range D1: D9 like this:

	D
1	**Data**
2	1
3	2
4	4
5	7
6	8
7	9
8	10
9	12

From data above, see table below for QUARTILE function examples:

| | | f_x | =QUARTILE(D2:D9;1) |

D	E	F	G	H
Data		quartile 1	3,5	
1		quartile 2	7,5	
2		quartile 3	9,25	
4				
7				
8				
9				
10				
12				

Pic 9.5 Quartile function

9.14 RANK

The rank function returns the rank of a specific number from. The syntax is:

RANK(number,ref,[order])

The number is mandatory, this is the number you want to find the-rank. Ref argument refers to array or reference to an array. The order will define the order type. If order = 0 or omitted, data will be sorted in descending order. If order = not 0, it will be sorted in ascending order.

For example, there is data in range A1:A6 like this:

	A
1	Data
2	7

3	3.5
4	3.5
5	1
6	2

From data above, see table below for RANK function examples:

Formula	Description	Result
=RANK(A3,A2:A6,1)	3.5-th rank from data above	3
=RANK(A2,A2:A6,1)	Rank for num = 7 from data above	5

9.15 SMALL

SMALL function return k-th smallest value from dataset/array. The syntax is:

SMALL(array,k)

If array empty, SMALL function will return #NUM! error. If k ≤ 0 or k > dataset's count. SMALL will return error #NUM!. If n = data count in array, SMALL (array,1) = smallest data, while SMALL(array,n)= largest data.

For example, data in range A1: B10:

	A	B
1	Data	Data
2	3	1
3	4	4
4	5	8
5	2	3
6	3	7
7	4	12
8	6	54
9	4	8
10	7	23

See table below for SMALL function examples:

Formula	Description	Result
=SMALL(A2:A10,4)	The 4th smallest value in the first column.	4
=SMALL(B2:B10,2)	2nd smallest value from the second column.	3

9.16 STDEV

STDEV function estimates standard deviation based on samples. Standard deviation is a unit for measuring how dispersed values from the mean. The syntax is:

STDEV(num1,[num2],...])

STDEV assumes that the arguments are population's sample. If you assume that arguments = all of the population, use STDEVP function instead.

STDEV use formula below:

$$\sqrt{\frac{\sum (x - \bar{x})^2}{(n-1)}}$$

Where x = sample's mean that can be calculated using AVERAGE(num1,num2,...) while n=sample's size. For example, there is data in range A1:A11 below:

	A
1	**Strength**
2	1345
3	1301
4	1368
5	1322
6	1310
7	1370

8	1318
9	1350
10	1303
11	1299

See table below for STDEV function example:

Formula	Description	Result
=STDEV(A2:A11)	Standard deviation from metal's strength	27.46392

9.17 STDEVP

STDEVP similar with STDEV, it's used if arguments = represent all population. If the sample size is huge, STDEV and STDEVP will returns similar value.

STDEVP use formula below:

$$\sqrt{\frac{\sum (x - \bar{x})^2}{n}}$$

You can see table below for STDEVP example:

Formula	Description	Result

=STDEVP(A2:A11)	Standard deviation from metal's strength. It's assumed that only 10 goods made, so the data become the population's data.	26.05455814

9.18 TREND

TREND function returns linear trend. This use least square method from y_knowns and x_knowns. This can return y in line for new x.The syntax is:

TREND(y_knowns,x_knowns,x_new,constant)

See example below for TREND function example:

A	B	C
Mon th	**Costs**	**Formula**
1	133,890	=TREND(B2:B13,A2:A13)
2	135,000	
3	135,790	
4	137,300	

5	138,130	
6	139,100	
7	139,900	
8	141,120	
9	141,890	
10	143,230	
11	144,000	
12	145,290	
Bula n	**Formula (Cost Prediction)**	
13	=TREND(B2:B13,A2:A13,A15:A19)	
14		

9.19 VAR

VAR functino returns variance based on sample. The syntax is:

VAR(num1,[num2],...])

Argument num1 is mandatory, VAR assumes that all of the arguments are population's sample. If data represent all of population, you can use VARP function.

VAR function arguments can be numbers, names, array or references to number.

Error value arguments cannot be converted to number, and will create error.

VAR use formula following formula:

$$\frac{\sum (x - \bar{x})^2}{n}$$

See following table for STDEV function example (the data used are the data in STDEV function example):

Formula	Description	Result
=VAR(A2:A11)	Metal's strength variance	754.2667

9.20 VARP

VARP similar to VAR, but VARP used if the data represents all population. The formula used in VARP:

$$\frac{\sum (x - \bar{x})^2}{n}$$

For example, if only 10 products created, you can use VARP to calculate the variance of the population:

Formula	Description	Result

=VARP(A2:A11)	Variance of population	678.84

In spreadsheet documents, texts are very important. Because what you write are texts, text can be used to give comments, etc. that is why excel have lots of text-related functions. Most important texts are explained in this chapter.

10.1 CHAR

CHAR function returns character based on ASCII value. The syntax of CHAR function is:

CHAR(ascii_value)

For example, there are values in range A1:A2:

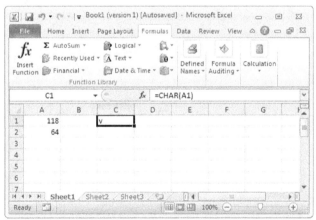

Pic 10.1 CHAR function

See the following table for CHAR function examples:

Formula	Description	Result
=CHAR(A1)	Returns CHAR from content of A1	"v"
=CHAR(A2)	Returns Char from content of A2	"@"
=CHAR(72)	Returns char from ASCII 72	"H"
=CHAR(109)	Returns char from ASCII 109	"m"

10.2 CLEAN

CLEAN function cleans all non-printable chars from a text. You can clean texts imported from other apps to excel, for example, from The Web that cannot be printed on your operating system.

The syntax is:

CLEAN(texts)

Pic 10.2 CLEAN function to clean non-printable chars

For example, there are data in range A1:A2

	A
1	Data
2	=CHAR(7)&"mytext"&CHAR(7)

See table below for CLEAN function example:

Formula	Description	Result
=CLEAN(A2)	Clean non-printable in CHAR(7)	mytext

10.3 CODE

CODE function will return ASCII value from char or first char in the cell. The syntax is:

CODE(text)

For example, data in range A1:A2:

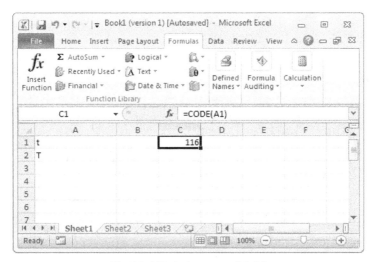

Pic 10.4 Data in range A1:A2

See the following table for CODE function examples:

Formula	Description	Result
=CODE(A1)	Returns ASCII from char in A1	116
=CODE(A2)	Returns ASCII from char in A2	84

10.4 CONCATENATE

CONCATENATE function concatenates strings as a single string. You can add up to 255 strings. String inserted can be a number, cell reference, or a combination.

Here's the example to concatenate the content of A1, space, and the content of B1.

    =CONCATENATE(A1," ",B1)

The second argument is space string to give space between two strings. The syntax is:

    CONCATENATE(text1, [text2], ...)

The mandatory is text1, the rests are optional.

							f_x	=CONCATENATE(D2; " ";E2)

C	D	E	F	G
	string1	string2	CONCATENATE	
	Wahana	Komputer	Wahana Komputer	
	Joko	Subianto	Joko Subianto	

Pic 10.5 CONCATENATE function

10.5 DOLLAR

DOLLAR function converts number to text using curency format. The format used is $#,##0.00_);($#,##0.00).

The syntax is:

    DOLLAR(number, [decimal_number])

The number argument is mandatory, while the decimal number is optional. For example, data in range A1:A2:

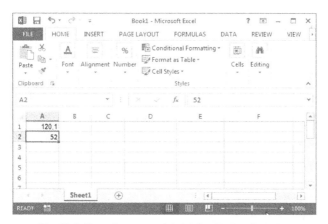

Pic 10.6 Data in range A1:A2 for Dollar function

See the following table for DOLLAR function examples:

Formula	Description	Result
=DOLLAR(A1, 0)	Create dollar from A1 with decimal = 0	$120
=DOLLAR(A1, 2)	Create dollar from A1 with decimal = 2	$120.10
=DOLLAR(1345, 2)	Create dollar from number = 1345 with two decimals.	$1,345.00
=DOLLAR(A1+A2, 2)	Create dollar with 2 decimals using addition of A1 and A2	$172.10

10.6 EXACT

The exact function compares 2 strings and decides whether they are identical or not. If identical, it will return TRUE, if not will return FALSE. The syntax is:

  EXACT(text1, text2)

The parameters just 2, first text and second text. See the following pic for EXACT function example:

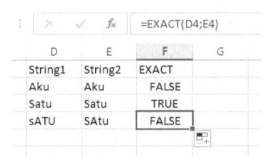

Pic 10.7 EXACT function example

10.7 FIND

FIND function returns location of a substring inside the string. The syntax is:

  FIND(substring, string, [first_position])

For example, data in range A1:A2:

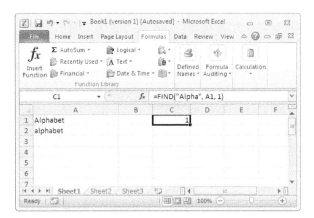

Pic 10.8 Data in range A1:A2

Formula	Description	Result
=FIND("Alpha", A1, 1)	Find string "Alpha" from string in A1	1
=FIND("alpha", A1, 1)	Find string "alpha" from string in A1	#VALUE!
=FIND("alpha", A2, 1)	Find string "alpha" from A2	1

10.8 FIXED

FIXED function returns text representation from a number, rounded to a certain decimal position. The syntax is:

FIXED(number, [decimal_position], [without_comma])

Without_comma is optional, if this parameter set to TRUE, the result won't display the comma. If set to FALSE, the result will display the comma. See the following pic:

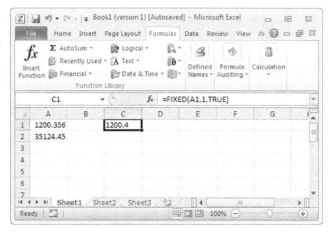

Pic 10.9 FIXED function

See table below for FIXED function examples:

Formula	Description	Result
=FIXED(A1, 1, TRUE)	Create fixed from A1 with one decimal.	1200.4
=FIXED(A1, 1, FALSE)	Create Fixed from A1, with one decimal, without_comma set to FALSE	1,200.4
=FIXED(A2, 0, TRUE)	Create FIXED from A2 with decimal_position = 0 and without_comma = TRUE	35124

10.9 LEFT

The left function returns a substring from the string, starts from the left side. The syntax is:

LEFT(text, [char_count])

See the following pic for LEFT function example:

	A	B	C	D	E	F
1						
2						
3		TEXT	LEFT			
4		First	Fir			
5		Excel	Exc			
6		NICE INFO	NIC			
7		Windows 10	Win			
8						
9						

Pic 10.10 LEFT (text;3) function

10.10   LEN

LEN function returns characters' count from strings. LENB return byte that represents a string. The syntax is:

LEN(text)

LENB(text)

See the following table for LEN function example:

Formula	Description	Result
=LEN("ADI")	Length of string	3
=LEN("Aku Cinta")	Length of string	9

10.11   LOWER

LOWER function returns the lowercase of string argument.

Lower (text)

Just enter the string argument, the function will be lowercase.

E11			×	✓	fx	
	A	B	C	D		E
1						
2						
3		TEXT	LOWER			
4		First	first			
5		Excel	excel			
6		NICE INFO	nice info			
7		Windows 10	windows 10			
8						

Pic 10.11 LOWER function returns lowercase of string argument

10.12   MID

MID function takes substring in the middle of the string. You can specify start position and length. The syntax is:

=MID(text;start_position;length)

See the following pic for MID function example in Excel:

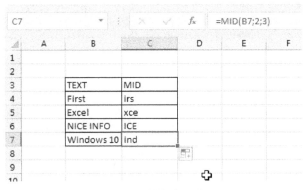

Pic 10.12 MID function

10.13   PROPER

PROPER function removes the bad form of a string, such as capitalization, more than one spaces, etc. The syntax is:

=PROPER(text)

See the following pic for PROPER function example:

C4			f_x	=PROPER(B4)	
	A	B	C	D	E	F
1						
2						
3		TEXT	PROPER			
4		FirstClass	Firstclass			
5		exCeLLL	Excelll			
6		NICE INFO	Nice Info			
7		WiNDOWs 10	Windows 10			
8						
9						

Pic 10.13 PROPER function

10.14   REPLACE

REPLACE function replaces part of a string with other strings. The syntax is:

=REPLACE(text, start_position, length, replacing_text)

See the following pic for REPLACE function examples:

Pic 10.14 REPLACE function

10.15   REPT

REPT function repeats texts for a specific number of repetition. The syntax is:

=REPT (text, repetition_number)

See pic below for REPT function example:

Pic 10.15 Repetition of string using REPT function

10.16   RIGHT

RIGHT function takes a substring of string from the right side. The syntax is:

   =RIGHT (text, char_count_from_right_side)

See pic below for RIGHT function examples:

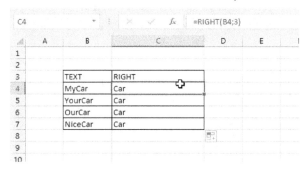

Pic 10.16 RIGHT function example:

10.17   SUBTITUTE

SUBSTITUTE function used to change substring with other replacement_string. The syntax is:

   =SUBSTITUTE (text, string, replacement_string)

See the following pic for SUBSTITUTE function example:

Pic 10.17 SUBSTITUTE function

10.18   T

T function returns the value after checking whether the value = text or not. If not, will return an empty string. The syntax is:

=T(value)

See the following pic to see whether the range D2:D5 have texts or not using T function.

Pic 10.18 T function example

10.19   TEXT

TEXT function converts a numerical value to text and enables you doing formatting using special strings. This function used to make the numerical value more readable in the report.

The syntax is:

=TEXT(cell,formatting)

For example, you want to combine number in cell A1 with text or symbol, you can use the following function:

=TEXT(A1,"$0.00")

See pic below for TEXT function example on formatting number to text with Indonesian currency format:

Pic 10.19 TEXT function

Lots of formatting available in this TEXT function, see the following table:

To display	As	Use This Format
1234.59	1234.6	"####.#"
8.9	8.900	"#.000"
0.631	0.6	"0.#"
12 1234.568	12.0 1234.57	"#.0#"
44.398 102.65 2.8	44.398 102.65 2.8 (with decimal)	"???.???"

| 5.25
5.3 | 5 1/4
5 3/10
(with fraction) | "# ???/???" |

See the following table for thousands formatting:

To Display	As	Use this format
12000	12,000	"#,###"
12000	12	"#,"
12200000	12.2	"0.0,,"

See the following table for months formatting:

m	**Display month as number without zero**
mm	Display month as a number with prefix = 0 if needed.
mmm	Display month in short form (Jan to Dec).
mmmm	Display month in full form (January to December).
mmmmm	Display month in one letter (J to D).
d	Display day as a number without prefix = 0.

dd	Display day as a number with prefix = 0 if needed.
ddd	Display day in short form (Sun to Sat).
dddd	Display day in full form (Sunday to Saturday).
yy	Display year in two digits.
yyyy	Display year in four digits.

For hour formatting, see the following table:

To display	As	Use this format
Hour	0–23	"h"
Hour	00–23	"hh"
Minute	0–59	"m"
Minute	00–59	"mm"
Second	0–59	"s"
Second	00–59	"ss"
Time	4 AM	"h AM/PM"
Time	4:36 PM	"h:mm AM/PM"
Time	4:36:03 P	"h:mm:ss A/P"
Time	4:36:03.75	"h:mm:ss.00"

Time (hour and minute)	1:02	"[h]:mm"
Time (minute and second)	62:16	"[mm]:ss"
Time (second)	3735.80	"[ss].00"

To insert some currency character, you can use key combinations below:

To Enter	Use Key Combinations
¢	ALT+0162
£	ALT+0163
¥	ALT+0165
€	ALT+0128

10.20   TRIM

The trim function removes more than one spaces between words, this will makes only one space exists between word. You can use the TRIM function to make texts imported from other sources eg: web, have nice space between words.

The syntax is:

=TRIM(text)

See following pic for TRIM function example:

Pic 10.20 TRIM function example

10.21   UPPER

UPPER function returns uppercase form from text argument. The syntax is:

=upper(text)

See pic below for UPPER function example:

Pic 10.21 UPPER function example

10.22   VALUE

VALUE function converts string that represents number to numerical value. The syntax is:

=VALUE(text)

See pic below for VALUE function example:

| | C7 | | | ▼ | : | ✕ | ✓ | *fx* | =VALUE(B7) | |

◢	A	B	C	D	E
1					
2					
3		TEXT	VALUE		
4		1300	1300		
5		9:10:10	0,382060185		
6		09/01/1990	32882		
7		8:45	0,364583333		
8					
9					

Pic 10.22 VALUE function example

See table below for VALUE function examples:

Formula	Description	Result
=VALUE("$1,000")	VALUE from "$1,000"	1000
=VALUE("16:48:00")-VALUE("12:00:00")	Serial number that equals = 4 hour and 48 minutes, "16:48:00" minus "12:00:00" (0.2 = 4:48).	0.2

ABOUT THE AUTHOR

Ali Akbar is an IT Author who has more than 10 years of experience in the architecture and has been using IT for more than 15 years. He has worked on design projects ranging from department store to transportation systems to the Semarang project. He is the all–time bestselling IT author and was cited as favorite IT author. Zico P. Putra is a senior engineering technician, IT consultant, author, & trainer with 10 years of experience in several design fields. He continues his PhD in Queen Mary University of London. Find out more at https://www.amazon.com/Zico-Pratama-Putra/e/B06XDRTM1G/

CAN I ASK A FAVOUR?

If you enjoyed this book, found it useful or otherwise then I would really appreciate it if you would post a short review on Amazon. I do read all the reviews personally so that I can continually write what people are wanting.

If you would like to leave a review, then please visit the link below:

https://www.amazon.com/dp/B07173FLGK

Thanks for your support!

www.ingramcontent.com/pod-product-compliance
Lightning Source LLC
LaVergne TN
LVHW022315060326
832902LV00020B/3485